How Executors Avoid
Personal Liability
A handbook for executors and beneficiaries

Lynne Butler, LAWYER

Self-Counsel Press
(a division of)
International Self-Counsel Press Ltd.
Canada   USA

Self-Counsel Press acknowledges the financial support of the Government of Canada through the Canada Book Fund for our publishing activities.

Printed in Canada.

First edition: 2014

Library and Archives Canada Cataloguing in Publication

Butler, Lynne, author

    How executors avoid personal liability / Lynne Butler.

(Legal series)

Issued in print and electronic formats.

ISBN 978-1-77040-193-8 (pbk.).—ISBN 978-1-77040-944-6 (epub).—ISBN 978-1-77040-945-3 (kindle)

    1. Executors and administrators—Canada. 2. Liability (Law)—Canada. I. Title. II. Series: Self-Counsel legal series

KE833.L5B87 2014	346.7105'6	C2014-900645-4
KF779.L5B87 2014		C2014-900646-2

Self-Counsel Press
(a division of)
International Self-Counsel Press Ltd.

North Vancouver, BC	Bellingham, WA
Canada	USA

Contents

Notice to Readers

Laws are constantly changing. Every effort is made to keep this publication as current as possible. However, the author, the publisher, and the vendor of this book make no representations or warranties regarding the outcome or the use to which the information in this book is put and are not assuming any liability for any claims, losses, or damages arising out of the use of this book. The reader should not rely on the author or the publisher of this book for any professional advice. Please be sure that you have the most recent edition.

Dedication

This book is dedicated with thanks to everyone who reads my blog, buys my books, and attends my seminars. Your questions have fueled my passion for Wills and Estates law for 30 years.

Introduction

You are an executor. Most of us who act as an executor do so only once in our lives, and for most, once is plenty. The person who named you as his or her executor probably intended it to be an honour for you, but it may not always feel that way once you start the actual work. It can be a tough job. There are stacks of unfamiliar paperwork, and endless discussions with lawyers, accountants, land title clerks, and bankers. There are countless questions from family members, not all of which you know how to answer. There are laws to learn and new procedures to follow.

The majority of executors are completely unprepared for the job in the sense that there is no official training for it and they have to feel their way along as they go. Who could blame you for wondering what you have gotten yourself into?

It is also true that beneficiaries are becoming more willing to consult the courts when an estate grinds to a halt due to what they may feel is executor mismanagement. At one time, estates were considered private family affairs and, at times, privacy was maintained at the expense of proper estate administration. Litigation is no longer seen as an embarrassment or failure; these days it is regarded more as a necessary tool. Any executor should realize that a shift in attitude such as this could well affect how the beneficiaries of an estate will react to the executor's behaviour.

By now you may have read the will that appoints you and have a general idea of what you need to do as executor. Or, if there is no will, you are the person who is going to step forward to be appointed by the court as the estate administrator. You are considering your options, doing some research, and perhaps hiring a lawyer to help you. You may already have heard or read that as an executor or administrator, you may be personally liable for mistakes you make while administering an estate: Any financial loss to the estate by the executor may result in the executor repaying that loss out of his or her own pocket.

One of the most complicating factors in any estate is that the people involved are likely emotionally volatile. Everyone, most of the time including the executor, has just lost someone dear to them and has been thrown into an unwanted situation. Family members are grieving and emotions are easily triggered. The executor ends up being blamed for everything that happens, even when that is completely unfair. This makes an already intimidating job even more challenging for an executor.

It can be pretty difficult under these conditions to carry out your duties as executor in a way that pleases everyone. However, this does not mean that you are doomed to endure months of harassment at the hands of the beneficiaries, or to end up in a lawsuit. It does not have to be that way. There are several steps that you can take to ensure that you do not regret taking on the executor's role or becoming the most hated person in the family.

This book looks at the ways that you, as an executor or a court-appointed estate administrator, may conduct yourself in a way that will not result in you becoming personally liable for your actions when looking after an estate.

We will also look at several of the ways that executors and administrators tend to get into trouble, with explanations of exactly what can go wrong. We will then discuss ways to avoid those particular minefields. This book contains information, examples, tips, and ideas that executors can use. The last chapter of the book contains some additional liability-reduction tips that are wonderfully effective, but so little-known and so underused they could almost be considered secrets.

Many of the problems and struggles encountered by executors during the estate administration are with the beneficiaries of the estate. You will notice as you read this book that the beneficiaries loom large in the majority of the issues raised. However, this does not mean that conflict with the beneficiaries is the only source of executor liability. In this book we will look at how co-executors may cause liability for each other. We will also touch on how an executor can become liable to third parties.

In this book, the word "executor" will mean either an executor named in a will, or a court-appointed administrator. In almost every respect, these jobs are the same once they are underway. However, administrators can incur liability in additional ways that executors cannot. Chapter 15 is dedicated to court-appointed administrators to cover a few issues that relate strictly to them, and not to executors named in wills.

What you will gain from using this book:

- You will gain knowledge of the most common mistakes executors and administrators make without realizing they are causing a problem. You will be able to head off problems before they start by being aware of the issues that are likely to arise and how your decisions and actions will either aggravate them or prevent them.

- You will gain an understanding of the various ways in which the courts deal with executors who break the rules intentionally, or who accidentally make mistakes. You will realize the importance of carrying out your executor's duties to the best of your ability by comprehending how seriously the legal system will consider any breach.

- You will gain practical ideas and information about how to avoid conflict and errors when working as an executor. This book will go beyond telling you how not to do things; it will provide information about how to proceed the right way.

- You will gain knowledge of the laws and legal processes with which an executor must deal. This book will help you focus on the areas that most need your attention at a time when you may feel overwhelmed with new information and responsibilities.

- You will gain the confidence you need to deal with an estate effectively and to manage the expectations of the beneficiaries. You will know that the beneficiaries have confidence in your abilities because you are showing them confidence, compassion, and leadership.

- You will know how to protect yourself from personal liability when acting as an executor. You probably agreed to act as executor because you felt it is your duty to do so. This book will help you carry out that duty without regretting your decisions.

Because this book is about liability, it must of course focus on financial losses that you as an executor might cause to an estate. However, there is another way in which you and the beneficiaries may well lose if you cannot properly discharge your duties as an executor: the emotional cost of family disharmony.

The number of families adversely affected by the fraudulent, negligent, or arrogant behaviour of an executor is simply staggering. The majority of families end up in a dispute of some sort during an estate administration. Some break up completely and are never mended. Often, this is the direct result of the actions of the executor.

While this kind of loss is important and worthy of consideration, it is not measurable in terms of money. It is not going to end up in court. The consequences are personal, not legal. This book will concentrate on keeping you out of court and out of the lawyer's office as a result of financial losses and legal mistakes. The added benefit of family harmony that will result from a smooth estate administration is a significant bonus.

There are endless variations on estates. Each is unique in terms of assets, liabilities, family, beneficiaries, and documents, and as a result there is no limit on the mistakes available for you to make. However, the mistakes tend to fall into general categories as we will discuss in this book.

It is important to realize that many mistakes by executors are made by honest, well-intentioned people just like you. While there are some executors who behave as if they have personally won the lottery when they are made executors, most take it more seriously than that. Most want to do a good job. It is easy to make a serious error, even when you are honest and paying attention, simply because you are not aware of a law, regulation, form, or process.

Some rules and laws that govern estates do not make a lot of sense to people who do not work with those rules often. In particular, executors and beneficiaries alike will complain that the estate taxation rules seem difficult to understand. This may be the case if you do not know the theory behind them, but as an executor you are probably not very interested in learning tax theory; all you likely want to know is how not to fall on the wrong side of the law.

Congratulations on choosing this book; you are already ahead of the game, since many executors do not even realize they may face personal liability until they are standing in a courtroom and wondering how they got there. By reading the descriptions and examples in the following chapters of the mistakes that executors frequently make, you will be able to avoid them yourself.

1
General Laws and Rules for Executors

In this chapter, you will find a brief review of the laws, regulations, and procedures that set out how an executor must behave in Canada. All statutes (written laws) that apply to wills, probate, and estate administration are provincial, so there are surprisingly wide differences between them. However, the general rules and principles are the same across the country. In the downloadable kit that accompanies this book, you will find a list of the laws that apply to each province and territory.

Laws regarding taxation of estates are made federally so they are the same for all Canadians.

The goal of this chapter is to guide you towards greater understanding of your role as executor and to help you find the resources you need.

1. Where Does It Say That?

A question asked over and over again during estate administration is, "where does it say that?" This question is asked by executors who have read the will thoroughly and simply do not see where it tells them that they cannot commingle (mix) the estate money with their own, or that they must wind up the estate in one year, or a hundred other things.

You may not see these things written in the will. In fact, it is highly unlikely that you will. However, they exist and they affect you.

A legal document of any kind, including a will, is prepared in the context of the laws of the land that relate to that document. An executor who is administering a will is expected to educate himself or herself as to the duties, rights, and obligations of an executor, no matter what is written in the will. You have to make it your business to find out which laws and regulations govern estates and executors, and to abide by them. Saying that you did not know the law will not help you if you are sued.

Therefore, realize right from the beginning that the will is a summary of what you must do, and the laws of your province and of Canada fill in the details of how you must do it.

2. An Executor Is a Type of Trustee

Words used in a will have definitions that are well-entrenched in law, because wills have been around for many hundreds of years. Our Canadian laws are based on British laws and processes that go back to the years before Canada existed in its current form.

These definitions bring with them legal rights and responsibilities that may be invisible to you when you read the will, but that exist in any event. For example, if you asked an average person to define the word "executor," you would probably hear something like "the person who looks after the will and pays everyone their inheritance." That is true as far as it goes. However, there is much more to it, as the word "executor" has been used in legal cases for hundreds of years. The law says that an executor of an estate is considered to be a trustee and must behave as a proper trustee.

Because an executor is a trustee, a mistake made by an executor is usually referred to as a breach of executor's duty.

Every province and territory has a *Trustee Act* which governs the rights and responsibilities of an executor or estate administrator. You might not know it from simply reading the will, but those obligations apply to you. It would be a good idea for you to read the *Trustee Act* for your province. Guidance that is typically found in a provincial *Trustee Act* includes:

- How an executor may or may not invest estate funds.

- Whether an executor may delegate his or her investment decisions to an advisor.

- How and when a substitute executor may be appointed, if that becomes necessary.

- How an executor can request to be removed as executor.

- Rules for selling the estate's real property.

- Information about the liability of executors.

- How an executor may use trust funds to look after a minor beneficiary.

- How an executor is to deal with creditors of the estate.

This is not an exhaustive list by any means, but these examples should be sufficient to indicate just how important the *Trustee Act* is to an executor. It contains valuable instructions and definitions which affect the executor. By agreeing to be an executor, you are agreeing to work within all of the rules and guidelines set out in this Act, even if you do not see those rules set out in the will.

Links to provincial *Trustee Acts* can be found in this book's download kit.

Each province and territory has its own laws, rules, processes, and forms that apply to wills, trusts, and probate matters. The will you are administering must be interpreted within those guidelines. Always ensure that any reference material you use is relevant to your particular province and is up to date.

3. An Executor Is a Fiduciary

Executors, by definition, are fiduciaries. This legal term refers to anyone who holds property, money, or information for someone else and who has a duty towards the person or people for whom those assets are held. This aspect of being an executor is arguably the most important characteristic of the executor's job. It will give rise to most of the complaints and questions about executors, even though the word "fiduciary" most likely does not appear in the will. This is because by accepting the job as an executor, you have accepted the fact that you owe a duty of loyalty to the estate, even when that loyalty conflicts with your best interests.

Some professionals, such as lawyers, accountants, bankers, and brokers, are also fiduciaries, and there are rules in place to ensure that they use the assets of an estate for the right purposes.

An executor is in conflict of interest if he or she cannot reconcile his or her personal interests with that of the estate, or if it appears to others that they cannot be reconciled. Few people can really overlook his or her own wishes when it comes to an estate. This may make it difficult to fulfill the fiduciary duties required.

A commonly seen example of an executor who is in a conflict of interest position is that of a spouse or child of the deceased who is the executor, but who wants to make a claim for a larger portion of the estate. The conflict arises because it is the executor's job to represent and defend the estate when any claim is made. It is impossible to sue the estate and defend the estate on the same lawsuit. An executor who is in a conflict of interest should step down as executor because it is impossible for him or her to properly act as a fiduciary.

Another important issue for executors that arises from their positions as fiduciaries is that of improper delegation. The general rule is that an executor cannot delegate his or her discretion. In other words, the deceased has asked you to step into his or her shoes to make decisions; you cannot then ask someone else to make those decisions.

We know that executors are allowed to hire people to help with an estate. As an executor, you may hire someone to help you carry out the decisions you have made, but you must be careful not to cross the line into letting others actually make the decisions for you. Executors are allowed to delegate tasks that are purely administrative, which allows you to hire a lawyer to apply for probate, an accountant to prepare a tax return, or a realtor to sell a property.

The key to avoiding liability when delegating these tasks is that you must make the decision to obtain probate and to place the values on the estate. You must decide that a return needs to be filed. You must decide that a property is to be sold and decide whether any particular offer is to be accepted. You have the responsibility and the liability for those decisions.

There is also a "reasonability" test. This means that executors are allowed to hire agents for assistance where it is reasonable to do so. Not every estate is complicated or large in value, and not every task is complex. An executor should only hire an agent when it is reasonable to do so in the circumstances of a particular estate. As a general rule, the courts have agreed that it is reasonable for executors to hire financial advisors or money managers to assist with investments, so you will not be held liable for delegating the management of a portfolio to them.

Executors and administrators are also affected by Canada's income tax laws, whether or not those laws are mentioned in the will.

This is because our *Income Tax Act* specifically says that any legal representative (which includes executors and administrators) is responsible for any taxes that are not paid if the legal representative pays out the beneficiaries before paying the tax. Again, this is something that you may not see in the will, but you are expected to find out when you start acting as an executor.

4. Common Law

Other rights and obligations for executors and administrators are not always written down in a rule book anywhere. They have developed over the years from what we call the "common law." This refers to a history or accumulation of cases that have been interpreted and decided by our courts (and before them, the courts of England). We rely on those cases as having set precedents, so that we can extrapolate the findings of those cases to our own situations. The reliance on precedent is intended to guide, interpret, and control the actions of executors, administrators, beneficiaries, creditors, and claimants.

Provincially, only Québec does not use the common-law system; it has its own legal system known as a civil-law system.

An example of a common-law rule that affects executors is the concept of the executor's year. This concept means that unless there are difficulties or complexities in an estate, the executor should be able to finalize it and pay out the beneficiaries within a year. It sets a goal for the executors, and it also alerts the beneficiaries not to expect the job to be done overnight.

The fact that a rule arises from a common-law precedent and not a written statute (except in New Brunswick where the one-year rule is set out in the *Devolution of Estates Act*) does not change the fact that an executor must abide by it, and may face consequences if he or she does not do so.

5. Summary of the Executor's Responsibilities

The following is a summary of the responsibilities of the executor that are created by statute and by the common law:

- The executor must follow the will.
- The executor must be impartial and fair towards all beneficiaries.
- The executor must protect and maximize the assets of the estate.
- The executor must give information as needed to beneficiaries, tax officials, creditors, agents, and third parties.
- The executor must delegate only matters that are appropriate.

- The executor must act in good faith.

Those general responsibilities each break down into several dozen individual tasks to be completed by an executor. In the downloadable kit included with this book you will find a more detailed list of executor's specific duties for you to use as a checklist as you work on your tasks as executor. When using the checklist, you should realize that as each estate is different, not every item on the list may apply to your situation.

6. Specific Language in a Will

It is important to realize that the powers and limitations of an executor as described in the previous sections of this chapter exist, but may be changed or augmented by specific language used in a will. The general rule is that the existing law is used as the default position unless it is varied by the will itself.

Not every wish or instruction given by a testator in a will is legal or binding. Sometimes testators will include clauses that simply cannot be followed, such as a man leaving a gift to his daughter only if she divorces her husband, or one that requires someone to repay an inheritance to the estate if he picks up the habit of smoking. If the will you are administering contains any unusual clauses like these, you should take the will to a lawyer for a discussion of how to handle the instructions.

However, most instructions left in a will that are intended to override the usual way of doing things are valid and should be followed. A few examples of clauses that validly direct the executor to manage things in a way that is outside the usual are:

- Directing that the beneficiary who inherits an asset pays the tax on that asset. Normally the taxes are paid by the general estate, regardless of who receives the taxable asset. This means that in the absence of any specific instructions, one person might inherit the deceased's cabin, while all beneficiaries have to bear the tax burden from the cabin. Sometimes testators who are aware of the way tax rules work will include a clause in the will directing that the beneficiary who gets the cabin (or business, land, or other taxable asset) will pay the taxes. As an executor, it is essential that you understand the source of tax payments, so pay close attention to any instructions in the will that reference payment of taxes.

- Directing that the share of someone who predeceases the testator is not to be shared among the deceased's children. We are used to seeing wills that say the inheritance of a person who has died should be paid to that person's children instead. In fact, this concept is the basis for intestacy law in most of Canada. However, if the will says that the inheritance is not to be divided among that person's children but is to go somewhere else instead, those instructions are valid.

- Directing that the entire estate be liquidated and the money divided. These days it is rare to see an estate that is completely sold off. However, if a testator wants that to happen with his or her estate, and sets out these instructions in a valid will, you are obligated to follow it.

7. The Executor's Powers Provided by the Will

The quality of any given will depends on the expertise of the lawyer or other person who drew it up, as well as the circumstances under which the will was prepared. Wills that are done hurriedly, such as death bed wills, may be simpler and may even be prepared without the benefit of legal advice. Some testators use will kits or forms found on the Internet; this can work quite well if care is taken to select a form for the right jurisdiction and if the kit's instructions are carried out properly. Mistakes can be made, whether or not a lawyer has been involved.

The best wills contain paragraphs that are referred to as "executor's powers" or "executor's authorities." When you begin working as an executor, you should read the will carefully to note which powers are provided for you. The purpose of these powers is to smooth the administration of the estate by allowing the executor to take certain steps without needing the permission of the beneficiaries or of the court.

As mentioned, the quality of wills varies. The better the quality of the will, the more you, as executor, are protected. This is because the lawyer who drew the will would have anticipated the steps you are going to take to administer the estate and would have included the specific powers you need to do that. In an estate where there are no disputes or struggles, the powers may be less crucial, but in most estates, the executor must rely on the powers for his or her legal authority to carry out certain tasks.

Even though federally it is implied that administrative tasks may be outsourced by the executor, some of the specific powers that you should be able to find in the will you are administering are:

- Power to sell real estate.

- Power to make income tax elections.

- Power to hire agents such as accountants, lawyers, or realtors.

- Power to give items to beneficiaries in specie, which means the ability to give a beneficiary an actual item without having to sell the item and give the beneficiary the funds.

Some wills need more powers than others, based on the needs of the person whose will it is. For example, a person who owns a business should have a will that allows his or her executor to carry on the business until the company is sold, and to deal with corporate matters such as registry filings and corporate resolutions.

When there are minor beneficiaries of the estate, further powers are needed to let the executor know who may handle money on behalf of the minor.

The lack of these powers in the will is a tricky situation for executors. Where the powers are present in the will, you can carry out the steps you need to take based on the will. Where the powers are absent, local law often requires either the written consent of all of the beneficiaries, or an order of the court allowing you to take the step. Be cautious when you want to carry out steps for which there is no specific power given. You may wish to consult a lawyer for an opinion on whether you have the legal authority to take steps such as:

- Selling, winding down, or carrying on a business.
- Selling a home even though there is enough money in the estate to pay the debts without selling the home.
- Rolling over an RRSP or RRIF to a spouse.
- Settling a lawsuit or claim on behalf of the estate.

2
An Executor Must Follow the Will

Though the heading "an executor must follow the will" seems straight-forward, a failure to do so includes a whole variety of ways in which you can get into real trouble. Executors do not always understand — or perhaps, do not want to accept — that the will is the foundation of the estate. It is not simply a document that confers a title of authority on him or her; it also contains important instructions for an executor to follow. Doing anything else amounts to paying the wrong amounts to people, which creates liability for the executor.

1. Making the Will "More Fair"

One scenario that is shockingly common is that of an executor who decides that the will "isn't fair" and decides to distribute the estate in a way not set out in the will. Typically, this happens in a family when one sibling is made the executor. He or she may think it is unfair that every-one gets the same amount under the will when one sibling was a care-giver to the parent for years and received nothing for it. Or, he or she might decide that it is not fair that one person is supposed to receive more than another person, since their parents loved all of them equally.

Executors and beneficiaries alike may be confused when they see a will that, on the face of it, treats the beneficiaries differently, when over the years they have heard their parents say that everyone would be treated equally. They forget that their idea of what it means to be treated equally simply may not be the same as that of the parent. They may not know everything that transpired between the parents and each child.

Rearranging the distribution in the name of improved fairness may also arise in a blended family. An executor who is a member of the deceased's first family may decide that it is not fair that some of the estate goes to the second family, or vice versa. Occasionally, executors who are children of the first marriage attempt to ignore their parent's wish to leave a part of the estate to the new spouse. Blended families can be a minefield of estate litigation because of executors who get caught up in emotional issues of what is and is not fair.

Sometimes executors overlook the fact that on intestacy, all biological children of the deceased are included in the distribution to children. If the deceased had a child of a previous marriage, or had a child out of wedlock, that biological child is entitled to the same share as a child who was born in the deceased's current marriage. This is true even where the deceased had little or no contact or relationship with that child.

Despite the fact that an executor can convince himself or herself that this is reasonable, it is not. It is neither the executor's will, nor the executor's money, and therefore it is not the executor's decision to make about what is fair. Like it or not, the executor's job is to carry out the instructions contained in the will and not to change them to suit his or her own values.

An executor who changes a will to make it "more fair" runs a very substantial risk of being sued by someone who is left out in the cold by the reconfiguring of the estate distribution. In fact, a lawsuit against you is all but guaranteed in that circumstance. If you have been named as an executor but feel that you simply cannot deal with an estate because it is just so unfair in your mind, then perhaps you should decline the job altogether.

2. Giving Personal Items to Those Not Entitled to Them

Another situation that is distressingly common is when the executor allows family members or others who are not named in the will to select personal items from the deceased's home as a memento. Though this sentiment is usually well-intentioned, it is not within the executor's authority. If you allow this, the beneficiaries have a right to object, and you should expect to pay for those items out of your own money.

This is a tough one for many executors. You may be pressured by family members who will play on your sense of fairness and loyalty to family members. You may end up feeling guilty and tight-fisted if you refuse to give a Royal Doulton figurine to a niece or the power tools to a grandson, even though those individuals are not named under the will. Try to remember that although it may please that niece or grandson to be included, your actions will likely upset someone else.

Not all wills contain specific instructions on how to deal with household and personal goods. The best wills contain a separate paragraph or two that give directions as to who may share in the division of household items. Usually this will include giving the executor the power to resolve a dispute when two beneficiaries want the same item. Remember that if household and personal goods are not specifically mentioned in the will, they become part of the residue of the estate and belong to the residuary beneficiaries. They are not yours to give away.

If two beneficiaries want the same item from the estate, you must resolve the dispute. Take care to use a method of resolution that is fair to both people and shows no favouritism on your part. Flipping a coin is acceptable.

3. Not Following Trust Instructions

On occasion, an executor is directed by a will to set up a trust for an individual. The reason for a trust described in the will you are administering may or may not be obvious to you from the will itself. Most people realize that trusts are required for underage beneficiaries and individuals who are mentally challenged. Many people also know that trusts can be set up for people who are not very good at handling money. However, there may be any number of reasons that the deceased wanted a beneficiary's share to be held in trust.

Trusts are sometimes set up because the deceased wanted to protect the beneficiary from creditors, or from a spouse in a shaky marriage. The deceased might have wanted to preserve an asset for another beneficiary after the first one. Perhaps the trust was set up so that the beneficiary would not be moved up to a higher tax bracket. You may not know the reason for the trust, but you are still required to set up the trust as directed by the will.

If the will directs you to set up a trust, it is not up to you to decide that a trust is not really needed. That decision simply is not within an executor's authority.

Beneficiaries are sometimes annoyed or even angry that their inheritance is to be held in trust. They take it as an insult. They make comments such as "I'm not a minor, and I'm not disabled, so why can't I have my money now?" They will pose the same question to you, the executor, and will exert a great deal of pressure on you to simply hand over the inheritance.

Before you give in to that pressure, consider this situation. Say the will instructs you to hold $100,000 in trust for Roger until he turns 30. Roger is now 22. The will contains the usual wording that Roger may have access to the money for medical or educational expenses at any time before then. Neither you nor Roger can see any obvious reason for the trust, so you pay it out to him.

However, every trust is written with instructions on what to do with the money if the beneficiary does not reach the age set out for receipt of the money. Say, in this case, that the will says that if Roger passes away before age 30, Roger's sisters will receive the money in the trust.

Let us say that Roger dies at age 28 in a car accident. His sisters then step forward to claim the $100,000. The funds are no longer in trust because you paid them to Roger, who left them in his will to his wife. You would be liable to the sisters for the $100,000, plus interest.

The only safe route for you is to set up the trust as directed by the will. There are some parts of estate distribution that may be changed if all beneficiaries agree in writing, but this is not one of them. If there is a good reason to challenge the money being in the trust, you may approach the court and ask for permission to do so. However, you should be aware that courts in general do not like to second-guess the testator's reasons for the trust.

4. Ignoring Parts of the Will

Similar to ignoring trust instructions, this section refers to an executor who decides to follow only the parts of the will that are convenient. An example of this is an executor who really does not feel like working with a co-executor, so simply ignores the part of the will that appointed the second executor and does not tell anyone about it. This has been tried by some executors, but they are always found out.

Executors have also been known to ignore sections that they do not believe to be fair (as discussed in section **1.**). For example, an executor might not want to sell the family farm even though that is directed in the will, or may not wish to pay out a bequest to a charity. The fact that the executor wants to farm the land himself or herself, or does not approve of the named charity, is simply not good enough.

As an executor, you must carry out all directions given in the will, even if some of them are not what you would have done had the property been yours.

5. Acting while the Testator Is Still Alive

A fact that does not always seem to be clear to those named as executors is that they have no authority under a person's will until that person has passed away. A surprising number of people will attempt to look after a parent's estate while the parent is still alive. These executors state that they are allowed to sell Mom's house or distribute Dad's bank account because of their appointment as executor.

These individuals in fact have no legal right whatsoever to access the parent's assets. They likely have the roles of executor and Power of Attorney confused. Only a person named under a Power of Attorney document may deal with a person's assets while that person is still alive.

Many an executor has experienced frustration, confusion, and even anger when banks, lawyers, realtors, and financial advisors refuse to help them deal with the parent's assets while the parent is still alive. The simple solution, if the parent still has mental capacity to deal with legal documents, is to advise the parent that in order to provide help sooner rather than later, the executor will also need to be named under a Power of Attorney.

When you think about it, this makes perfect sense. Nobody can sell our assets, because we own them. The fact that we have named someone to do something for us in the future does not allow him or her to take, sell, or distribute what we own now. Executors who are the children of aging parents often do not seem to be able to step back and see their parents as individuals with rights that exist outside the family. They tend to think that because they are the children of that person, they can usurp that person's rights when that person gets older.

The law simply does not allow this. Being someone's child does not give you any right to dispose of his or her property. Being named as someone's executor does not give you any rights while he or she is alive. You must still follow the law, even with your parents.

3
An Executor Must Obtain Valuations

When you are dealing with monetary assets such as bank accounts, bonds, or investments, it is easy to ascertain the value of the asset simply by looking at a statement from the financial institution. You are entitled to rely on a current, bank-generated statement as being accurate. Other assets are not as easy to valuate.

As an executor, you are liable for the loss to the estate if you sell an asset for less than it is worth. You are also liable if you give something away or throw it away thinking it is worthless, and it later turns out to have value. You must be very careful to understand what you are dealing with in an estate and to place correct values on all assets.

Wherever possible, get appraisals or estimates to back up the value you put on assets. For example, when you sell a house or other property, you would do well to get at least one appraisal first. Many executors obtain two or three appraisals and average them out to determine the selling price. You must sell at fair market value. If you do not, you could be held liable for the difference a beneficiary may not have received as part of his or her inheritance, if that person decides to take you to court. The more expensive or complex a property, the greater the chance that at least one beneficiary will believe that you have sold it too cheaply. If the beneficiaries are already arguing about this, or if one of them wants to buy an estate property, protect yourself by getting two or three appraisals.

Where an estate is modest and it just does not make sense to hire an appraiser, you should at the very least get estimates from local realtors. These can be obtained at no cost. Two or three valuations by realtors are better than one. Get these in writing and keep them to demonstrate why you sold the property at a given price.

Also note that when you are preparing the estate inventory (the list of assets), the values you place on the assets must be the value on the date the person died. If on the day your mother died she had $15,000 in her chequing account and owed $1,000 on her Visa card, you must show both of those amounts on the inventory. If you have already paid the Visa by the time you prepare the inventory, that does not change anything. You must show the situation as it existed on the date of death.

It is also important to remember that when you prepare an inventory of the estate, which every executor must do, you will have to swear under oath that the values are accurate. Therefore you should do everything you can to ensure that you are not swearing to something falsely, which is also referred to as committing perjury.

1. Selling Major Assets below Market Value

If you are selling a vehicle, do a bit of research first to see the selling price of similar vehicles of similar age and condition. Look around to find the usual asking price for the vehicle. Do not just look at one classified advertisement or eBay offering; look at several so that you are confident you know the price is right. Keep these advertisements or printed web pages in your files to show how you arrived at the selling price. Quite often, there may be a nephew or a friend who would like to buy the car from the estate, which is perfectly alright. However, it may be tempting to sell the car at a reduced price, simply to give a family member a break.

Understand that if you sell the car, or any other asset, at a reduced price, there may well be someone involved in the estate who is not going to like it, for one reason or another. There is a way to protect yourself. If you would like to sell, say, a $10,000 vehicle to a young nephew who loves the car but is only offering $2,000, make sure you have written consent from all of the residuary beneficiaries.

When you sell an asset for less than fair market value, you are taking money right out of the pockets of the beneficiaries. They may not mind, if it means helping their young nephew get his first car, but make sure you have it in writing. A verbal agreement is not useful at all; make sure you have at least an email message that clearly shows the sender is aware that the price of the car has been reduced to help out a family member. If you have it in writing from all of them, nobody can criticize you for it later. This arrangement is known as beneficiary acquiescence, which is covered in more detail in Chapter 14.

It is not necessary for you to get permission from the beneficiaries to sell assets such as vehicles, boats, artwork, jewelry, or furniture. It is only required in the example above because the price was being reduced below what the car would have fetched on the open market. You can use this kind of arrangement to sell other assets, as well, if the beneficiaries are open to it.

It is not a good idea to sell a house or other real estate to anyone for below market value, because it may end up causing them a capital gains tax problem later on, depending on the circumstances.

2. Selling Household Items

One of the ways that executors get into trouble with valuations is by selling small assets, such as household and personal items, for less than they are worth. As a general rule, used furniture, clothing, kitchenware, and household knick-knacks do not have much resale value. Because of this, executors will almost always hold some kind of garage sale or estate sale to try to generate some small income from these items. This is perfectly acceptable, as long as you are extremely careful about the items you sell.

Most likely, nobody is going to mind whether you sell used paperback books for 50 cents or a dollar. The dollar value is simply too small for anyone to argue about. They are going to mind, however, if you sell Grandmother's sterling silver teapot for a dollar. Many an executor has been shocked to find that he or she has sold a valuable painting, antique chair, or gold jewelry for next to nothing at a garage sale. Upon the discovery of the loss of the value of the item, the executor is required to pay the real price of the items to the estate himself or herself.

The general rule for executors to know is that if you sell any item belonging to the estate for less than its market value, you are responsible for the monetary loss to the estate. To avoid finding yourself in this situation, take steps to ensure that you are charging an appropriate price. If you suspect that some of the old furniture or collectibles are antiques, consult a dealer and get an appraisal. If there is artwork of any kind, call a dealer to find out the value of the items. If you are not sure whether the silver teapot is real silver or just chrome, find out for sure before you place it on that garage sale table. Similarly, do not assume that all of the jewelry in the estate is costume jewelry; ask a jeweler whether the gems are real or not.

Look into any item that is unusual, rare, or specialized. The time spent may well save you thousands of dollars. Items that you should double check value on might include:

- First editions of books, or rare books.
- Coin or stamp collections.
- Sports memorabilia such as card collections or signed jerseys.
- Items made by a prominent company such as Tiffany, Waterford, or Lalique.
- Family heirlooms such as old photos, pocket watches, or service medals.
- Any items that are autographed.
- Pop culture items such as vinyl records or vintage posters.
- Original art including drawings, paintings, sculpture, etchings, carvings.
- Any items with historical relevance such as war medals, military uniforms or paraphernalia.

This is not to suggest that every item that is unusual or old has monetary value. However, to protect yourself, you should always take steps to find out an item's value.

3. Acceptable Methods of Sale

Assuming that you are comfortable with the values you have placed on physical estate assets, you may sell them in any manner that suits you and is reasonable in the circumstances. Some of your options for sale are:

- Garage sale or estate sale.
- Consignment to an auction house.
- eBay, Kijiji, and other auction or sale websites.
- Classified ads.
- Secondhand store.

- Collector who gave you the valuation.
- Word of mouth to friends, family, and neighbours.

It is worth stating that some items will have no resale value at all, such as most used clothing and household linens. As executor, you are entitled to make the decision that some common items have no value, and to dispose of them by giving them to a charity or throwing them away.

4. Calling on Experts

Do everything you can to identify and valuate items properly. As discussed in the previous section, you should bring in the help you need to make sure that you are not going to make a costly error.

It is not always possible to have someone come into the house, or for you to take the items in question to an expert. Not everyone has an antiques dealer and art gallery down the street. If you do not have the expertise you need close by, take good, clear photos of the items, write factual descriptions for them in terms of size, age, and condition, and find expertise online. You can send photos, together with your notes of the items to experts in almost any field. Using the Internet, the distance from you will not matter a great deal, though you should always bear in mind the cost of shipping the items if that becomes necessary for sale.

This is particularly useful when you need to place a value on something like a hockey card collection or a collection of old wax LP records, or something else that is important to a niche market.

5. Selling to Beneficiaries and to the Executor

Beneficiaries are just as entitled as anyone else to buy items from the estate. If there are items that have not been left to specific beneficiaries and the executor has listed them for sale, there is no reason that one of the beneficiaries may not purchase the items for fair market value. The executor should, of course, keep all paperwork relating to the sale so that he or she can establish that the right price was charged, that funds were actually received, and that no favouritism was shown.

When it comes to the executor buying estate assets, the situation is more complicated. An executor who wants to buy an asset from the estate is in a conflict of interest, as his or her desire to get the asset as cheaply as possible conflicts with his or her executor's duty to get the best price possible for the item.

Some wills provide guidance on this issue by stating that the executor may purchase assets from the estate. If this is present in the will that you are administering, you may buy property or items from the estate without court permission. You should be very careful when setting the sale price so that you do not risk being accused of shortchanging the estate. Keep the purchase transaction above board and as transparent as possible. Keeping the details secret or confusing will only cause speculation among beneficiaries about what you are hiding.

If the will does not specifically allow you as executor to purchase assets from the estate, and the majority of wills do not, you should ask the court for permission to do so. This involves asking for approval not of the general idea of buying something from the estate, but of a specific purchase of a specific item at a specific price.

Court permission is most often applicable when an executor wants to buy real estate, as opposed to household objects or vehicles, from the estate. If this is your situation, make sure that you can demonstrate to the court through evidence that you are paying a fair price. This would be done by getting independent appraisals (more than one is best) of the property.

If you obtain court permission to purchase a property, the beneficiaries will not be able to complain later on that the deal was not fair. At the time you apply to the court for permission, any beneficiary who objects to you buying the asset should be given notice of your court application so that the objections can be heard and dealt with.

4
The Executor Must Communicate with Beneficiaries

Lack of communication is by far the most common complaint that beneficiaries have about executors. Beneficiaries complain that they are not being informed of the steps being taken, or why things are happening (or more likely, why they are not happening), or what is going on with particular assets. The more they are kept in the dark, the more upset they become, and very soon they have turned to suspicion and speculation.

Before long, the beneficiaries may become convinced that you are hiding something, that your spouse is persuading you to keep estate assets for yourself, that you have hired a crooked lawyer, and that the whole estate is a mess. If they cannot get the information they want from you, often the next step they take is to hire a lawyer to challenge, or at least examine, what you are doing. Suddenly you may be involved in a lawsuit.

While this is the most common mistake executors make, it is also the simplest to prevent.

As an executor, you do have to keep beneficiaries informed. You cannot change that just because you find it inconvenient or you do not like some of the beneficiaries. There is no question that certain beneficiaries have the legal right to know everything that is going on. You are looking after their money, so of course they are entitled to know what you are doing with it. If months go by without you giving them any information, they will not know what you are doing. You may be working feverishly on the estate each and every day, but if you do not tell them, they will not know about it. It will look to them as if you are secretly carrying out your personal agenda.

Keep in mind that executors are sued just as often for the perception of unfairness or wrongdoing as they are for actual unfairness or wrongdoing. Standing back and telling yourself that nothing bad is going to happen because everything you are doing is above board is not enough; you may still be perceived as being in the wrong if you do not communicate.

In dealing with beneficiaries, you are going to have to strike a balance. No executor has time to field five or six calls every day from beneficiaries. If you are already finding it challenging to find the time to fit in your executor duties around your family, home, and work, being overwhelmed by calls and emails is not going to improve matters. You should take control of this situation as soon as possible.

You can, as they say, kill two birds with one stone. You can reduce calls and emails, and also reduce the chance that someone is going to be so upset with your lack of communication that you are served with legal process to appear in court.

The first step is to understand who is entitled to information, and what exactly they are entitled to receive. This will help you to determine with whom you need to communicate and how much you may say. The second step is to decide upon an effective and efficient way of delivering that information.

1. Showing the Deceased's Will to Family Members

Most executors are asked by family members to show them the will of the deceased. This is a hugely emotional topic for someone who asks you for this, so treat it professionally. Not everyone is entitled to see the will, and part of your responsibility to the deceased person you represent is to protect his or her privacy. You simply cannot give out copies of the will to individuals who have no business seeing it. Only residuary beneficiaries of the estate are entitled to see the will. A person is not entitled to see the will just because he or she is related to the deceased, even if he or she is a child of the deceased. This is a hard message to deliver to someone, and even harder to hear, but you may have to be the bearer of that unpleasant message.

To understand who is a residuary beneficiary, check the wording in the will. The residuary beneficiaries are those who share in the bulk of the estate. Usually you will see words like "the residue of my estate," or "the rest of my estate," or simply "divide my estate among the following persons." In older, more old-fashioned wills, the language can be convoluted and much more difficult to understand, and you may end up asking the estate lawyer to help you with this.

To illustrate this point, let's say that Alfred makes a will that leaves the following:

- $5,000 to his church;

- $5,000 to each of his old friends, Marty and Jane; and

- Everything else divided between his children, Anna and George.

In this scenario, only Anna and George are the residuary beneficiaries. Marty, Jane, and the church are called specific beneficiaries, and they are not entitled to read the will. They are entitled to see only the paragraph in which their gift was left to them.

Along with the right to see the will, the residuary beneficiaries are entitled to see everything else in the estate. They are entitled to examine the records you keep and all of the documents you file for the estate. The reasoning for this difference in the right to see the will and other estate information is simple; residuary beneficiaries cannot know what they are to inherit if they cannot see what is happening with the estate. They do not know what the rest of the estate is going to be without that documentation.

It is very common among executors, for some reason, to prefer to keep every scrap of information relating to the estate secret. One of the most frequent questions asked of estate lawyers is how to get an executor to release the information to which a beneficiary is entitled.

Taking this secretive stance is not beneficial to you as the executor, or to the estate. In fact, it is almost sure to create a lawsuit. Once you establish everyone's status as either a residuary beneficiary or not, you need to understand your duty to report to them.

It may be the case that a family member is absolutely certain that he or she is a beneficiary under the will and demands that you give him or her a copy of the will, even though that person is in fact not named in the will. If you are like most executors, you will make the mistake of simply ignoring this person on the basis that as a non-beneficiary, he or she is not entitled to a response. This is not the right approach. Send the family member a letter, politely confirming that you have read the will and that he or she is not a beneficiary. That will at least give the person an explanation.

2. Proactive Communication

The estate is going to run more smoothly for everyone if you accept that there are certain people to whom you must answer, and that those people may aggressively pursue you for information.

Take a proactive approach. Advise the residuary beneficiaries early on that they are residuary beneficiaries, and that you will keep them informed on a regular basis. Then stick to that promise. A good way to structure this is to set up an email distribution list that is just for residuary beneficiaries. Tell them that in the early stages of the estate when a lot is happening, you will report to them once a week. Make it clear to them that you simply cannot and will not field individual calls from them, because you just do not have enough hours in the day. You are offering them a deal: A weekly report in exchange for peace and quiet.

Your weekly report does not have to be fancy or lengthy. Point form would do. You might say, for example:

- "I received an appraisal on the house for $350,000. I'm getting another one on Tuesday."

- "Does the 12th work for everyone to get together and divide up the personal items Mom left in the house?"

- "I opened the safe deposit box at the bank, and found Canada Savings Bonds worth $5,000. I've cashed them and put them in the executor's bank account."

- "I applied for the CPP death benefit."

- "Probate has been filed; the lawyer says it will take about three weeks."

Though you might groan at the idea of having to sit down each and every week and summarize your activities when you are already busy, you should understand that this will take up a lot less time than constant calls, emails, texts, and visits. You will not have to repeat yourself as many times. There is less chance of misunderstandings if the information is given to beneficiaries directly by you and not passed around by each other. The most important thing you achieve by using this process is to ensure that no beneficiaries begin to lose faith in you and suspect you of hiding something, so you are much less likely to be sued.

Keep your reports honest. If there is a delay or a problem, include that. If the wording in the will is contradictory and needs to be sorted out by a judge, say so. If you find out that the estate is going to be reduced significantly because the deceased had not filed tax returns for the last ten years, tell them. If you miss an appointment with the lawyer or accountant because you were sick that day, just say so. There is no point trying to hide things.

As the estate progresses, there will be less activity to report, so simply advise in one of your later weekly emails that you are going to reduce your reports to biweekly or monthly.

If there is a beneficiary who does not use email, ask one of the other beneficiaries who lives nearby to that person to print out your email message and drop it off to him or her. Alternatively, you could ask one of the other beneficiaries to call that person and read your message to him or her.

5
The Executor Must Not Mismanage Estate Assets

Mismanagement of estate assets is another area in which there are many possible mistakes made by the executor. Many errors of this type are made by executors who really are trying to administer the estate correctly but quite simply do not know what steps to take.

Many of these mistakes could be prevented by consulting with a lawyer, banker, or financial advisor to find out what you are supposed to do. This chapter will give you a head start on knowing what problems are out there.

1. Mingling Estate and Personal Funds

One of the most critical errors you can make as an executor is to treat the estate's money as if it were your own. You need to remember this basic rule of executorship at all times: It is not your money. You are only the custodian of it.

Unfortunately, some executors are unable to resist the temptation to treat estate funds as personal play money. These executors have shored up the finances of their own failing businesses, lent money to their children, or played the stock market. Others move into the deceased's home or farm the deceased's farm and simply do not want to move out because the arrangement works for them financially.

All of these executors have one thing in common: They were all sued. They each ended up in a lawyer's office looking for costly legal representation because they were being sued by the beneficiaries of the estate they were representing.

There are legal meanings, rights, and obligations attached to the specific words used in a will. Non-lawyers may not recognize those nuances, and get into trouble because they do not follow them.

In 1999 the courts in Nova Scotia heard the case of *Crouse Estate v. Saunders*. In that case, the executor used some of the estate assets of a value of about $130,000 for his own use. The beneficiaries objected, but the executor took the position that the law allows an executor to use the estate funds in the same way as the testator could have done himself. He pointed to words in the will that seemed to say that he could do so. In other words, he said in a surprisingly arrogant statement that he could not be removed as executor unless he was first convicted of theft. The court recognized this as the twisting of words that it was, removed the executor from his job as executor, and ordered him to repay the funds.

The executor appealed the decision twice and lost both times. The courts each time said that it was absolutely clear law that the executor could not treat estate assets as his own. The executor ended up paying his own legal costs for his court applications.

When the law says, as it does, that an executor can do anything with estate funds that the deceased could have done, it means that assets can be sold, invested, and transferred. However, all of these transactions must be made by the executor in the best interest of the estate and not of himself or herself.

2. The Executor's Estate Bank Account

You should be scrupulously careful to make sure that you never mingle the estate funds with your personal funds or your personal business affairs. At best, this is a case of poor judgment; at worst, it is theft. As soon as there is anything to deposit for the estate, open an executor's bank account. This account may be opened where you bank or where the deceased banked, as you choose. Most executors find the greatest co-operation from banking personnel when they open executor's accounts at the deceased's bank.

The executor's account should not be opened in your name personally. It should be opened as, for example, "John Smith, the executor of the estate of Jane Smith." When you open the account, be extremely careful that it is opened correctly, as the proper name on the account will govern not only ownership of the funds, but the proper allocation of tax receipts.

Check the paperwork prepared by the bank before you sign to open the account. Occasionally, an estate account is incorrectly opened by identifying the executor as a power of attorney rather than an executor. This is legally incorrect and you should not allow the account to be opened in this way.

Do not allow anyone else to have access to this account, other than your co-executors, if there are any. Do not simply add the funds to your own account "for now" until you get around to opening a proper account. Do not make the account a joint account with your spouse to allow your spouse to help with the banking. Do not put the beneficiaries' names on as cosigners or joint owners. The money belongs to the estate until distributed, and you are its gatekeeper.

Remember that if any funds go missing from the estate, you will be held personally responsible for them. Opening an executor's bank account should not only help you with the administration of the estate, it should also protect you. You will have a way of ensuring that the estate money is never mingled with anyone else's money. Interest or dividends earned on estate funds will automatically be paid to the estate and not inadvertently added to anyone else's income. Using an executor's bank account keeps estate transactions cleaner and more transparent.

3. Investing Excess Cash (or Not)

Executors sometimes make the mistake of cashing in a GIC or selling the home, then keeping the proceeds in a bank account. If the proceeds are going to be paid out again quickly, this may not be a problem. However, if the funds are not going to be used for 30 days or more, you should ensure that they are invested.

If the funds are not invested, they will not earn a good rate of return. They will definitely earn less return in a bank account than they will in an investment portfolio, as interest rates are currently very low. If the funds could have grown but did not because you did not invest them, you may be held accountable for the amount that was not earned.

This is something you will have to decide for yourself by considering the amount of money, how long you expect it to be kept before you are ready to pay it out, and the cost of investing. If the cost of setting up an investment account and paying a money manager is more than the funds would earn, clearly you would not be criticized for not investing them.

3.1 Investing foolishly

Executors who invest foolishly may well be sued for the investment losses. It may not be immediately clear to all executors what is meant by a "foolish" investment. This refers to the level of care that is expected to be taken by the executor.

Each province and territory directs executors in the care of estate investments through its *Trustee Act*. Without exception, all provinces and territories refer to a standard of care called "the prudent investor rule." Though the wording varies slightly from place to place, it is always a variation on "the trustee may invest trust money in any kind of property, real, personal, or mixed, but in so doing, the trustee shall exercise the judgment and care that a person of prudence, discretion and intelligence would exercise as a trustee of the property of others."

This rule means that you can choose whether you invest in real estate, bonds, stocks, or mutual funds. The choice of specific investment instruments is wide open. However, your choice must make sense in the context of the market conditions, the expected length of time of the investment, and the needs of the beneficiaries. You are expected to be prudent; this is another word for careful. You have to pay attention to what the investments are doing. You should follow accepted investment practices as recommended by your financial advisor.

What this boils down to for the vast majority of executors is asking a professional for help. Unless you are a professional money manager yourself, you are probably not the right person to handle the investments for the estate. You are entitled to hire a money manager or financial advisor, and you are required to provide all of the information that person will need to make good investments on behalf of the estate.

As a general rule, executors are not allowed to delegate the parts of their role that require discretion. However, hiring a money manager does not involve delegating your discretion if you are the one who determines the goals and needs of the estate investments. Though you will hire the money manager to pick specific stocks or funds, you retain the responsibility for deciding whether the investments are doing what the estate needs them to do.

You also need to keep your wits about you. If an investment scheme sounds risky or crazy to you, you are responsible for walking away from it with the estate funds intact. Remember that the prudent investor rule refers to "the trustee of property of others," reminding you that you cannot take foolish risks with other people's money even if you do so with your own money. If you are sued for investment losses, you will not be protected by saying that you did not know what the money manager was doing.

4. Not Protecting Assets

You might as well accept that some decisions you make as executor are going to make you unpopular with family members. This may be because they do not see the reasons for those decisions, nor do they understand or accept that you are the one who will face the consequences if you do not stick by these decisions.

The decisions referred to are those that will bar family members from the access they are used to having to the family home, for example. If the estate includes the home of a parent who is now deceased, you should change the locks on the home as soon as possible. You are responsible for any items that disappear. As mentioned, family members may not see why they may not continue to stay at the family home, come and go as they please, and even help themselves to mementos. You have to put a stop to all of that.

You must check to make sure that the deceased's home is insured for fire, and if it is not, insure it immediately and keep it insured until it is sold or transferred. You must also make sure that you inform the insurers that it is vacant. If you fail to do this and there is a fire or other claim while the home is still vacant, the claim for coverage may be denied and you will be on the hook for the loss. While the house is in the estate, you must also make sure that you keep it in good repair.

All of the precautions that apply to the deceased's home also apply to any cottage or vacation property owned by the deceased. You do not necessarily know whether neighbours, caregivers, or family members have keys or know the security codes, so you must take control of these assets.

You must also make sure that anyone who has keys to the deceased's vehicle return them to you, and that you keep the vehicle insured until it is sold or transferred. If you allow someone to drive the deceased's vehicle and it is damaged, any uninsured damage will be charged to you. This may include public liability if the person driving the car has an accident.

As soon as you can, go to any safe deposit box owned by the deceased. List its contents in detail. If anyone else has access to the box, you may wish to take the items and place them in a new safe deposit box to make sure that the items do not disappear. You should also take any small, valuable items that you find in the house, car, or cottage into safekeeping. These items might include jewelry, small artwork, coins, or keepsakes. Again, the loss of these items could result in you being required to repay the estate for their value.

Go through the deceased's home and remove all paperwork, including non-financial documents such as identification cards and passport. Keep these documents secure and confidential at all times.

5. Paying the Wrong Creditors

It must be unbelievably frustrating for an executor to do his or her best to pay creditors of the estate in a timely manner, only to find out that this attempt has led to liability. It usually happens when the deceased has left debts which are being aggressively collected by a creditor. The executor wishes to avoid interest charges or late fees for the debt, and pays it as soon as estate funds are available, even though information about the estate is still coming in.

The problem is that there is a ranking system for debts of an estate. Some rank higher than others and must be paid first, even if they are not the ones making the most noise to be paid. If there is not enough money to pay every debt in full, an executor who has paid the wrong creditors is likely going to have to pay any shortfall out of his or her personal funds.

During the process of gathering information about the estate assets and debts, all creditors should be told that their information will be included in the estate accounting, and that payments will be made following the grant of probate and an examination of the estate as a whole. There is no question that some creditors and collection agencies are painfully annoying and aggressive, but you may tell them that you do not intend to budge until the proper time and that they are wasting their time harassing you.

You should ask creditors to suspend the accumulation of interest or late charges while you work on wrapping up the estate, but only some of them will agree to do this.

To protect yourself, do not pay creditors until you are satisfied that you have all of the information about the estate. The fact that someone left a large estate is not necessarily an assurance that there will be enough money to pay all creditors, as many people carry large debts as well.

An exception to not paying creditors is the payment of the funeral bill. You may safely pay this bill as soon as possible, as it ranks above all other debts of an estate. Make sure that the cost of the funeral, cremation, or other memorial services are reasonable in the circumstances. For example, if a deceased person leaves an estate of only $25,000, it is not really reasonable to spend $12,000 on the funeral. That kind of lavish funeral might be okay for a large estate, but it is too expensive in the circumstances.

As an executor, you may be on the hook for extravagant funeral expenses. If the deceased prearranged the funeral himself or herself, you may be protected by that prearrangement, especially if it was partially prepaid, but in every other case, keep costs reasonable. That does not mean that you have to order the cheapest funeral you can find; it just means you should use common sense.

Note that a grave stone or marker is not considered a funeral expense. If the family members want the estate to pay for a monument, get the agreement of the beneficiaries in writing before you go ahead.

If you find that the estate is not large enough to pay all of the debts and expenses as well as pay the beneficiaries, you may wish to get legal advice on who to pay, and from which beneficiary's share. You are not going to be able to make everyone happy, so the goal has to be to do the job by the book and have the law to back up your actions.

6
The Executor Should Get Professional Help with the Estate

You are not expected to know everything there is to know to carry out an estate administration without asking for help. There are very few people who know everything from tax laws to probate procedure to property appraisal. Those who do think they know all of that are rarely correct. You are allowed, and in fact, you are expected to call on experts to help you with the estate.

Some of the professionals you might seek include:

- A funeral home, undertaker, or crematorium.

- A lawyer to help you with probate and to advise on your legal obligations as an executor.

- A trust company to carry out estate administration (more on this in Chapter 17).

- Appraisers to give you valuations on land, houses, antiques, collections, and many other items.

- An accountant to prepare tax returns, to advise about deadlines and available tax elections, and to apply for a Tax Clearance Certificate.

- A financial advisor, broker, or banker to manage estate funds and to set up trusts.

- A realtor to sell property.

- Renovators or contractors to make repairs or upgrades to property in the estate, if this will increase the likelihood of a better sale.

- Cleaners or movers to clear a house in the estate.

You are entitled to hire assistance for some of the day-to-day tasks such as cleaning out the deceased's home. You should be aware though, that when you delegate tasks that would normally fall on an executor, your executor's fee should be proportionately reduced by the amount paid for that help.

Also keep in mind that by hiring third parties to help with the estate, you are entering into contracts with those people or companies. By law, you are personally responsible for making sure that the contracted parties are paid for the work you ask them to do. Therefore, make sure that the estate can afford to purchase the help you want, or you may end up paying for it yourself.

1. Be Reasonable

You may use estate funds to hire any of the service providers listed above, but there is a limit. This limit is not expressed anywhere in terms of a specific dollar amount, but only in terms of common sense. You may only use estate funds if the expenses are properly incurred on behalf of the estate. This means you have to be reasonable in terms of how you use the services and the prices you pay.

If you spend too much of the estate money on service providers, you may find that the beneficiaries will contest your accounting and executor fee, and you will end up repaying to the estate the amount you overspent.

In December of 2012, the Ontario Supreme Court handled a case in which the beneficiaries complained that the executor was taking too much in fees and overpaying other expenses (*Stephen Thompson Family Trust v. Thompson*).

The judge required the executor to pass his accounts in court. The beneficiaries had objected to 23 disbursements claimed by the executor, and the court examined each of the 23 items. As a result, the court disallowed 20 of the expenses and required the executor to repay these amounts to the estate.

The disbursements that had to be repaid included $14,000 to a lawyer, $31,000 to accountants, and $22,000 in overpaid executor fees.

The executor had to repay all of that out of his personal resources. The reason given by the judge was that the actions requested and paid for by the executor really did not benefit the estate at all, so there was no reason the estate should pay for them.

It is hard to imagine how one executor on one estate overpaid accountants by $31,000 and it is not surprising that the beneficiaries would object to having to pay that sum. The amounts in question are not always this large, but even if you had to repay half of what this executor was ordered to pay, it would be a challenge for most people to come up with the funds.

The lesson to be learned here is to work with professionals, but to question whether the work you are requesting really is of benefit to the estate. Always ask yourself whether you could justify the expense if ordered to account by a judge.

2. Asking the Court for Help

All executors have the right to go to the court and ask for advice on matters that are unclear. However, most executors do not realize they can do that, and even some who do realize it choose not to go that route. This can be a major mistake, as not every decision is within the executor's legal authority.

Most people interpret an executor going to court as an act of hostility. The beneficiaries may assume that because you are going to court, you are acting against them. This is a time for communication and co-operation. Make sure that the beneficiaries understand that you are in a neutral position, and that you are asking the court for help for the estate so that you may proceed legally and properly, to their benefit.

It is important that you always approach the court as a neutral party when you are asking for help. Do not advocate for a specific outcome, as no matter what outcome results, it will be more beneficial to one beneficiary than another, and the executor is not entitled to take sides.

3. Wording in the Will

You should ask the court for guidance if the will you are administering contains wording that is so unclear that you have to guess what you are supposed to do. As an executor, you do not have the legal authority to decide what the deceased meant; it must be clear in the will itself.

For example, the will might say to "give $5,000 to John and Mary." Without any other guidance in the will, you have to determine whether this means that John and Mary share the funds, getting $2,500 each, or whether they each get $5,000. Had the will been worded more precisely, you would not have to guess, but poorly drafted wills are common.

If you were to share the $5,000 between them, both John and Mary might be upset with you that they did not each get $5,000. They may feel that they did not get their whole share. On the other hand, if you gave them each $5,000, the residuary beneficiaries might be upset thinking that you had over-paid John and Mary, causing a shortfall for the residuary beneficiaries. Now add a zero to the end of the number in question, and you can see how easy it is to get into trouble.

This is a very simple example that illustrates that things can be read two ways, but in some cases the wording is even worse. Another common example is "give Frank my house to do with as he wishes, and when Frank passes away, give the house to Angela." The asset in question could be a house or a bank account or anything else, but the problem is the same: How can the deceased give the house to someone after Frank dies if Frank then owns it? Inconsistencies such as this are frequent in wills.

The only way that the deceased could maintain control of an asset is to set up a trust. In the example above, the deceased's will would have to put the deceased's home in trust for Frank so that he can use the house during his lifetime but not sell it. This is the only way the house could later be given to Angela. The estate would have to hold on to the title of the house, but that is not what the will says. In fact, the will seems to suggest that Frank is free to do whatever he wants with the house, including selling it. Also, if the house is to be held in trust, the will does not say anything about who is supposed to pay the property tax, the fire insurance, the mortgage, and the maintenance.

No matter how you read that sentence giving the house to Frank, it is not adequate. The only way to deal with this situation without one of the beneficiaries being unhappy with you and possibly willing to sue you is to ask a judge for clarification.

If you ask the court for an interpretation, you must approach the court neutrally, meaning that you are not trying to convince the judge of one interpretation or the other. It is inappropriate for an executor to take sides between beneficiaries, and in some cases the judge has cracked down hard on an executor who took a side. You should ask the judge whether you should hold the house in trust or not, and if you are supposed to hold it in trust, you could get some clarification about the expenses.

Note that beneficiaries will be made aware of the court application, and most likely will choose to participate so that they can present their side of the argument. Even if they do, you are to remain neutral.

Other examples of questions that a court might resolve are:

- Who is intended to be a beneficiary when a charitable organization is named in the will but no longer exists?

- Does intergenerational joint property belong to the surviving joint owner or the estate of the deceased? (See Chapter 8 for an explanation of and more about intergenerational joint assets.)

- Who exactly is in a group or class of beneficiaries, when the will includes groups such as "my children" or "my nieces and nephews"? There may be confusion about whether step-children, foster children, illegitimate children, or unborn children should be included in the group.

4. Matters in Dispute

Executors may approach the court for help when there is a dispute between parties that simply cannot be resolved through negotiation. One of the most common ways that an executor can ask the court for help is by asking for a passing of accounts when the beneficiaries will not agree to his or her accounting.

This section of the book does not mean to suggest that you should run to the court every time there is a question or a disagreement. Only approach the court about a dispute with the beneficiaries when there is simply no hope of resolving it and the estate is at a standstill because of it. There have been cases lately in which the courts have punished both beneficiaries and executors for being so unreasonable that they cannot seem to settle even the smallest disagreement.

Punishment for bringing frivolous or spiteful lawsuits just to flex your muscles is usually in the form of legal costs ordered by the judge at the end of the lawsuit or hearing. A clear example of this treatment happened in 2012 in the Ontario Court of Appeal in the case of *Smith Estate v. Rotstein*.

In that case, a woman challenged her mother's will on the basis that her mother lacked testamentary capacity and was unduly influenced into making the will. These are two grounds for contesting a will that are well founded in law, but they can be hard to prove without very strong evidence.

The woman's brother was the executor and was therefore required to defend the will. The woman lost in Supreme Court, and appealed the case to the Court of Appeal. By the time the case made it through two levels of court, the brother's legal bills were more than $700,000. Both parties — the executor and the contesting sister — wanted their legal bills paid out of the estate.

The judge felt that the lawsuit was carried on more out of spite than because of a real legal issue. He said that there was so little evidence supporting the woman's claim that she should never have brought the case in the first place. He also said that if she had brought the case in good faith, she should have dropped it early on once she saw all of the evidence. However, the woman stubbornly carried on with the lawsuit, apparently thinking that the costs would not matter because the estate would pay them.

The judge made the woman responsible for the brother's legal costs of $700,000, as well as for $30,000 in disbursements to beneficiaries because the judge did not believe the case was something that should have been doggedly pursued through the courts. This case makes it clear that pointless litigation just for spite will not be tolerated.

While in this case it was the beneficiary who received the brunt of the court's punishment, there was enough discussion of the behaviour of all parties to conclude that the judge was not particularly impressed with the executor either. The courts expect people to act as adults and to resolve disputes among themselves if at all possible. Where resolution is not possible despite rational behaviour on both sides, the courts will offer assistance.

7
The Executor Must Keep Proper Records

It is absolutely essential that you, as an executor, keep detailed records of everything you do with the estate. You should be prepared at all times to give a full accounting of your actions to the beneficiaries or the court within 30 days of being asked for it. This chapter will help you keep the records you need in a useful format. Get a folder immediately and keep every bit of paperwork in it. You may find that your folder becomes a set of accordion files or binders, if the estate you are working on becomes complex.

Also start a ledger or spreadsheet for all income and expenses for the estate. Sometimes executors skip this step because they think they will be able to use the bank statements from the executor's bank account as a record. However, you may be working on the estate before the account is opened. Also, bank statements do not usually contain nearly enough information about each individual transaction.

For example, a bank statement may show a deposit for $150,000 with no other information other than the date of deposit. If you use the bank statement as your accounting, the beneficiaries will ask you what that deposit is all about. And they are going to ask about every other deposit as well. By the time you get to the end of the estate, you will not be able to remember the details of each transaction. You would be better off to identify that $150,000 from the beginning. If this sum came from the sale of the house or the cashing in of a GIC, put that in your ledger. The more detail you include, the less likely you are to be bombarded with requests for more information.

Your ledger or spreadsheet can be set up on your computer if that is convenient for you. Alternatively, you may keep a handwritten record as long as it is legible to other people. Beneficiaries do not always react well to handwritten reports because they feel they are somehow less businesslike, but if you do not have access to a computer, go ahead and prepare a handwritten ledger. Use the format that you are realistically going to maintain on a regular basis. There is a format suggested in section **3**.

Once you are ready to wind up the estate, the records you have kept will form the basis of your final report. If you have kept sloppy or incomplete records, you probably will not be able to produce a worthwhile accounting. You can expect pushback from the beneficiaries if that is the case. You will spend time and energy explaining and defending your accounting.

Even if you are able to produce a decent accounting, it is going to take you twice as long and take twice as much work as it would have if you had simply kept good records in the first place.

1. Original Paperwork

Keep all original bank statements, correspondence, certificates, appraisals, receipts, invoices, vouchers, notices, work orders, cancelled cheques, and anything else that crops up while you are working on the estate. You do not have to attach everything to your accounting or regular reports, but at least if anyone challenges you, you will have the paperwork to support your decisions and actions.

Beneficiaries often complain that original receipts, cheques, and other paperwork are not attached to the accounting that you provide to them. They tend to believe that an executor's report is hiding something if the originals are not attached.

However, you are not required to attach the originals to your accounting. If there is a dispute or question about a specific transaction, you should provide the person asking for information with a photocopy or scanned copy of the original. There is no reason to release the original of any document to the beneficiaries, though of course you are entitled to show them the originals if you wish to do so.

It would be impossible to provide original paperwork to everyone who asks in any event, as there is only one original of each item. If you are asked to pass your accounts to the court, be prepared to produce the original paperwork.

2. Pay Bills and Taxes before Paying Beneficiaries and Yourself

You will notice soon after becoming an executor that the beneficiaries are very anxious to receive their inheritance. They want their money sooner rather than later. For some this may be greed, but for many it is simply the need to have closure after a parent's or friend's passing away. They will pressure you to hurry things, even when you are moving the estate along at a reasonable pace. The average beneficiary does not understand how labour-intensive estate administration can be.

You must be prepared to deal with this pressure to accelerate the estate so that you do not accidentally incur liability by paying the beneficiaries too quickly. Another of the unbreakable rules of executorship is that bills, expenses, and taxes must by law be paid in full before the beneficiaries receive anything. As long as you really are carrying out the estate administration as efficiently and quickly as possible, the beneficiaries will simply have to wait.

You can also charge a fee for your services as executor, as well as claim expenses such as some travel expenses, or outsourced administrative help; for more about how to compensate yourself as an executor, see Chapter 12.

In one of your regular reports to the beneficiaries, you should let them know that you are in the process of determining debts and estate expenses. Tell them that nobody should expect to receive anything until that process is completed, and that it will take some time.

If a deceased person passed away leaving more debt than assets, this could well mean that the beneficiaries will not receive anything at all, or might receive a reduced inheritance, as the estate funds will be used up in paying liabilities. That is not a happy message for the executor to deliver, but sometimes it is necessary.

If you find that debts and liabilities are going to eat up the whole estate, or a substantial portion of it, you are going to have to break the news to the beneficiaries. They will be disappointed and suspicious of you, and will expect you to prove it. Many beneficiaries who find out that they are not going to inherit what they expected to inherit are outraged, and become very angry with the executor. The fact that they may have overestimated the deceased's financial position generally does not occur to beneficiaries; they often assume that the executor has somehow embezzled the estate funds.

In a case like this, be patient. Understand that grief and shock make people say and do things they might not normally say or do, including blame you for something you have not done. Stay calm and try to see it simply as a business transaction, rather than be hurt or insulted. If you find yourself in a position in which you have to deliver disappointing news to the beneficiaries, you should be prepared to present a very detailed accounting to them. Show exactly what assets were there, and exactly what those assets were used for. This is not a time to play secrecy games or to refuse to co-operate, as you will end up in court if you do.

3. Setting up a Ledger

The ledger is the backbone of your record-keeping. It is simply a complete record of every transaction you make with estate assets. If you set it up properly at the beginning, you will be able to convert it quickly and easily into the final document you will present to the beneficiaries when it is time to account to them. See Sample 1.

The downloadable kit that accompanies this book contains a blank sample ledger that you can use in Microsoft Word format. If you are one of the many executors who would prefer to use a spreadsheet program, refer to the sample ledger to find out which column headings you will need to set up when you create your spreadsheet.

The ledger is not intended only to keep track of a bank account, though it will in large part correspond with your executor's estate account. In the ledger you will record all funds received by the estate, no matter the source, and all funds paid out by the estate. The ledger should include a running balance of the estate so that you know at a glance what is available for the payment of expenses, or for an interim distribution if that is something you feel comfortable doing (see Chapter 10 for more about interim distributions). Having a running balance is also convenient if beneficiaries request information about the estate assets.

You will find that it is worth your time to include specific information in the "details" column. Doing so will save you hours of trying to answer specific questions from beneficiaries, the accountant who prepares the tax returns, and a judge should your accounts be passed in the court. More information is definitely better than less.

As an example, let us assume that you cash in a Guaranteed Investment Certificate (GIC) that was owned by the deceased. Many executors would be tempted simply to enter the amount received and "GIC" in the details column. However, many months later the accountant will need to know how much of that amount was made up of interest earned. If you do not have that information in the ledger, you will have to spend the time to go back through your paperwork to find that information. A better option would be to include an entry such as what you see in Sample 2.

Keeping this kind of detail becomes even more important if there will be several similar entries, such as multiple GICs or bank accounts. This will help you to keep track of exactly which assets you have received and to answer questions from beneficiaries.

Sample 1
Executor's Ledger (Blank)

Executor's Ledger

The Estate of _____, Deceased

For the period from _____ to _____

Date	Received	Paid	Details	Balance

Sample 2
Executor's Ledger (Filled-In)

Executor's Ledger

The Estate of _____John Smith_____, Deceased

For the period from __Jan. 27, 2015__ to _____

Date	Received	Paid	Details	Balance
2015-01-27	$ 251,772		Proceeds of Scotia GIC #12345. Principal $ 245,000, interest $ 6,772	$ 251,772

8
The Executor Must Know the Law

Not every executor hires a lawyer, and from time to time that can be a problem. Not only can a lack of legal guidance cause delays as you try to figure things out on your own, but it can result in your making serious legal mistakes. You should be as informed as possible on the legal issues touching on the estate you are administering, whether or not you hire a lawyer. If you are working with a lawyer, this chapter may help you to focus on topics you may wish to raise with the lawyer. This chapter does not cover every possible mistake of law that could happen, as they would be nearly impossible to enumerate. However, it contains several examples of mistakes about the law that are commonly made by executors, so that hopefully by being made aware of them you can avoid them.

1. Loans, Gifts, and Advances Made by the Parents

Let's say an executor is administering a will in which his parent divided the estate equally among the executor and his siblings. The executor pays the bills and files the taxes, and decides that he is ready to distribute the estate. He knows that his parents gave his sister a large sum of money several years ago to help her buy a home. Because his sister said that the money was a gift and not a loan, he does not reduce his sister's share. He pays everyone an equal amount. The other siblings sue him for overpaying his sister.

This executor did not realize that he was supposed to deduct the money that his parents gave his sister as a down payment on her house. You, as executor, are required to collect any and all monies owing to the deceased at the time of the person's death. If you fail to collect a receivable, you may be required to repay those funds to the estate yourself.

Money given or loaned to a child by a parent while the parent is alive is considered in law to be an advance on the child's inheritance, and therefore is a receivable. That fact is not well known, and if you do not know it and therefore do not deal with money advanced to the kids by the deceased, you could be on the hook for the amount not collected.

Do not be surprised if this issue becomes explosive. The debate about whether the kids are supposed to repay the financial help they received from their parents is a lively one in many estates. When you tell one of the children they are receiving less from the estate because of the financial help they received in the past, he or she will not take it well, especially if he or she is your sibling. Nobody wants to hear that an inheritance will be reduced. You will likely be accused of being greedy and going against the will-maker's wishes.

Almost nobody documents money that is given to one of his or her children. Sometimes a loan (as opposed to a gift) will be documented, but even that is rare between parents and child. It seems that somehow it is seen as insulting or mistrusting even to suggest that the transaction should be recorded.

In just about 100 per cent of the cases, the child who received the funds will say that the parent told them it did not have to be repaid. Whether or not that is the case is irrelevant; the law says that it does. It makes no difference whether it was a loan or a gift to the child.

Obviously if the help given to the child was repaid by the child to the parents while the parents were alive, this rule simply does not apply. Once the money has been paid back, it is no longer in question.

If you find that in the estate you are administering, one or more of the children received a significant amount of funds from the parents, look first to the will. Check to see whether it says anything about repayment of loans or advances. This is something that experienced wills and estates lawyers will cover with their clients, but it is still the minority of wills that say anything about it.

If the will says that loans or advances are to be forgiven, you do not have to do anything about the funds given. You may tell the beneficiaries that the will instructs you not to collect the amount given to the child. The children who did not receive any help may resent this, but if you are following the law, that is not your concern.

If the will is one of the old-fashioned kind written in confusing legalese, look for the word "hotchpot." That is a legal term that was, and sometimes still is, used to deal with advances to the children. If it says that advances are not to be brought into hotchpot, it means the loans or gifts are forgiven and you do not have to deal with them.

Note that the word "advance" applies to any gifts or loans to the children. Often beneficiaries will bicker about the word "advance" because in their minds the funds were gifted, not loaned or advanced. However, "advance" is the proper legal term for funds given or loaned to the children while the parents were alive.

If the will says that an advance is to be brought into hotchpot, this means that the will is confirming that you have to deduct the loan or gift amount from the beneficiary's share. In practical terms, you do not have to ask the beneficiary to write you a cheque; you will simply reduce the inheritance to show that this particular beneficiary gets less.

When you are dealing with this issue, you may find the pressure and the quarrelling very hard to take. It will be tempting to give in to the pressure by the beneficiary who insists that he or she is not going to repay the advance because Mom or Dad said he or she did not have to. Be realistic about how you handle this. If you give in to the pressure and tell the beneficiary that it is okay not to repay it, you may well be on the hook for the full amount.

Keep this in context. If there is only one beneficiary of the residue, it makes absolutely no difference whether that beneficiary has had an advance. The reason behind repaying advances is to effect a fair distribution among all of the beneficiaries. If equalizing is not relevant because there is only one beneficiary, you will not have to worry about this issue.

The following is a formula for subtracting an advance from a beneficiary's share. There may be other ways of calculation that will arrive at the same result, but this is a tried and true method you can use if you wish.

In this example, assume that three siblings, Abe, Brian, and Carrie, are supposed to receive equal shares of an estate valued at $50,000. If they split it equally, they would receive:

- Abe $16,666
- Brian $16,667
- Carrie $16,667

Brian had received $9,000 from their parents a few years ago to help him buy a home. Now Brian must repay that amount to the estate. You will take the following steps to adjust for the $9,000:

1. Add the $9,000 to the $50,000 nominally. In other words, Brian does not have to actually repay the funds. This equation acts as if he had paid it back.

2. Divide the estate three equal ways.

3. Subtract $9,000 from Brian's share.

The new nominal estate amount is $59,000. If that were divided equally among the siblings, they would receive:

- Abe $19,666
- Brian $19,667
- Carrie $19,667

Brian's advance of $9,000 would be subtracted from his share, leaving the distribution as:

- Abe $19,666
- Brian $10,667
- Carrie $19,667
- Total: $50,000

This formula is important because there is one error that is frequently made by executors. That is, they deduct the advance and split it only among the other beneficiaries, with nothing going to the person who repaid the advance. Using that incorrect formula, in this example, Brian's $9,000 would be split between Abe and Carrie, who would each receive $21,166 while Brian would receive only $7,667.

Splitting the repaid advance only to the other beneficiaries is incorrect because the repayment of the advance is not supposed to be made to the other beneficiaries. Legally it is made to the estate. As Brian is an equal beneficiary of the estate, he receives an equal share of the amount he paid back. A person in Brian's position would rightly be upset with the executor for distributing the funds the incorrect way.

You will note that because dollar amounts do not always divide exactly among the number of beneficiaries, one of the beneficiaries may receive one dollar less than the others; you can assign that one dollar arbitrarily.

2. The Limitation Period for Dependent Relief Claims

An executor is administering her father's will, in which the estate is divided between the executor, her siblings, and her father's second wife. Things wrap up fairly quickly, and four months after her father's death, the executor pays out all of the beneficiaries according to the will. She does not realize that she is supposed to wait six months after probate because that is the time set by statute for the father's wife to make a claim for a greater share of the estate. The wife brings the claim on time, but now the executor has to explain to the judge why the money is no longer there to pay her. Since there is no explanation other than "I didn't know I was supposed to wait six months," the executor will have to pay the amount of the claim out of her own pocket.

Every province and territory in Canada has laws that are referred to as "dependent relief" laws. This refers to the fact that a person who makes a will is required to look after his or her financial dependents. If he or she does not adequately provide for those dependents, they may make a claim against the estate for a greater share.

You need to be aware of whether there is anyone in the estate you are administering that would qualify as a dependent for the purpose of this law. The people in question are:

- A spouse of the deceased.

- A minor child of the deceased.

- An adult child of the deceased who is disabled to the extent that he or she cannot earn a living.

This is the point at which you may need to consult a lawyer. It is essential that you know whether the estate may face a claim. It is particularly tricky when there are spouses involved, as the word "spouse" has different meanings in law from province to province.

In all parts of Canada, legally married spouses have the right to claim against the estate. In some parts of Canada, common-law spouses have that right as well, but not everywhere. At the time of preparing this book, the provinces that do not allow inheritance rights to common-law spouses are New Brunswick, Newfoundland and Labrador, Ontario, Prince Edward Island, and Québec. In all other provinces and territories, you should at least be aware that a claim by a common-law spouse is possible.

Also keep in mind that a claim from a married spouse can occur in any part of Canada, even when the spouses have been living separate and apart. When couples are in the midst of divorce or property division, you may well need a lawyer to advise you as to the spouse's rights under matrimonial law.

Dependent relief claims cannot occur when the spouse is given the entire estate. This makes sense as there is nothing else to claim once the estate is given in its entirety. However, if you are administering a will which divides the estate between a spouse and other beneficiaries, be aware that a claim by the spouse is possible. This is particularly common where the deceased had been married or lived common law more than once.

A person who is in a second or subsequent marriage and who has children from his or her first marriage will typically split the estate in a way that favours the children. This of course depends on the length of the second marriage as well as other factors, but it is very rare to see a person in a second marriage leave out his or her children from the first marriage entirely.

In a situation like this, the spouse may decide to claim against the estate on the basis that he or she has not been adequately provided for in the will. There could also be a claim by a disabled child or a minor child. These claims would be made in the form of a lawsuit in the probate court. You will not decide who gets what; the judge will do that. Your job will be to show up at the hearing and provide the judge with information about the estate. After the hearing, you will carry out the judge's instructions for division of the estate.

If the person who has a right to make a claim is willing to provide you with a waiver in writing, clearly indicating that he or she is not going to make a claim against the estate, you may proceed with the distribution of the estate without sitting out the full waiting period.

It is a good idea to consult a lawyer to discuss whether any of the individuals in the deceased's life have the right to bring a claim, and to find out how long you should hold on to estate assets by law. In the example above, the time limit is six months, but that may not be the same everywhere in Canada. It is better to err on the side of caution, as you do not want to end up paying thousands of dollars to a claimant just because you moved too quickly.

3. Intergenerational Joint Assets

Intergenerational joint assets are very problematic right now, because they are treated so inconsistently across the country. The law is clear on what is supposed to happen, but banks, brokers, and others has been slow to respond to the change in the law that occurred in 2007. Be extremely careful with assets that are jointly owned between the deceased and an individual who is a generation younger than the deceased.

Prior to 2007, any account or asset that was held in joint names between a deceased person and any other person was automatically presumed to be owned by the surviving joint owner. This was the law of survivorship that had always applied to any joint asset.

In 2007, the Supreme Court of Canada dealt with two cases (*Pecore v. Pecore*, and *Madsen Estate v. Saylor*) that resulted in a major change to the previous law. Now the law states that the joint asset is still joint if it is owned by the deceased jointly with his or her spouse, or by the deceased with a minor child. However, an account that is held jointly by the deceased and any other individual, such as an adult child, niece or nephew, grandchild, or common-law spouse, is presumed by the law to belong to the estate.

It is possible for the surviving owner of the account to bring evidence that will defeat the presumption that it belongs to the estate and, depending on the evidence, to allow the survivor to own the asset. Your responsibility as executor is to hold on to that account or asset until the evidence has been presented and there has been a determination about ownership.

This is a complicated situation for any executor to handle, in part because very few people other than lawyers and bankers are aware of this relatively new law. A surviving joint owner will assume that he or she now owns the asset and will not be pleased when you state otherwise. This topic is rife with disputes and you will have to tread carefully. Legally, you must take control of the joint asset, and safeguard it until you find out whether it belongs to the estate or to the surviving joint owner. If you allow the asset to be taken by the surviving owner when it is supposed to belong to the estate, and by extension the beneficiaries, you will be held liable for the amount of the asset.

You may not be able to work through this situation without the help of a lawyer. You may even end up taking the matter to court for a judge to decide.

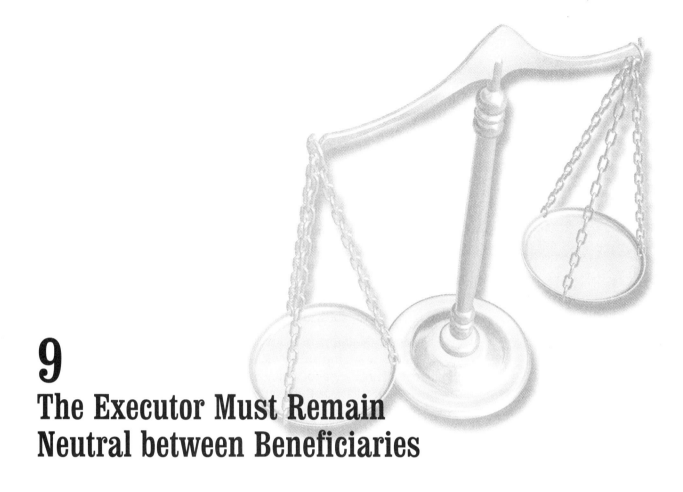

9
The Executor Must Remain Neutral between Beneficiaries

There is often confusion in an estate about who the executor works for. Beneficiaries often become irate when they find that the executor will not allow them to take their mother's sewing machine or their father's antique pocket watch. The statement from beneficiaries is usually along the lines of: "But we are the beneficiaries; the executor answers to us!"

While it is true that the beneficiaries are ultimately the ones who decide whether the executor has been honest and effective, it is not true that the executor has to do everything the beneficiaries ask. The executor's duty is to the estate as a whole, as directed by the will.

When a will divides an estate equally among a number of beneficiaries, or where intestacy law dictates that a number of beneficiaries receive equal shares of an estate, the executor's job is to ensure that equality is achieved. The executor cannot allow a beneficiary to take his father's antique pocket watch unless the executor is sure that this is supposed to happen under the will. The fact that the beneficiary claims a closeness with his parent and perhaps a lifelong interest in the pocket watch does not change things.

If the executor were to allow the beneficiary to receive the pocket watch without giving other beneficiaries an equal chance to claim personal items from the estate, the executor would be showing favouritism to one beneficiary. Not only is this a breach of the executor's duty, it is a surefire way to enrage the rest of the beneficiaries.

1. The Even-Hand Rule

There is a concept in law known as the "even-hand rule." This refers to the fact that an executor has a legal duty to remain neutral between beneficiaries of an estate. This is also known as the "duty of impartiality." Even when a trust is written so that the executor has a lot of discretion, he or she must remain impartial, and maintain an even hand between the individuals involved.

This sounds simple in theory, but in practice, remaining impartial can become a swamp of suspicion and complaints by beneficiaries. Some complaints are about things which have very little substance. For example, beneficiaries often complain that the executor chose a lawyer who is friends with one of the beneficiaries (not the one doing the complaining, of course). If you are sure that you have chosen a competent lawyer for the job, then this is a complaint that you may not want to bother to address. This is particularly true in small towns where there are not a lot of lawyers and accountants from which to choose.

Other complaints have more merit to them. Beneficiaries frequently state that an executor allowed one of the other beneficiaries to go into the family home and take items from it without affording the same opportunity to the rest of the beneficiaries. A variation on that complaint is that the executor allowed his or her own children or spouse to take items from the house, drive the deceased's car, or live in the deceased's home.

2. Favouritism, or the Appearance of It

You must realize that not only do you have to be scrupulously fair, but you also have to be seen as being scrupulously fair.

You should change the locks on the deceased's home as soon as possible and not allow any beneficiaries (or anyone else who might help himself or herself to a household item) to go into the home without first arranging it with you. Make every effort to be fair, and make every effort to be obvious that you are being fair. The best idea for distributing household items is to have everyone attend at the house at the same time so that they have equal opportunity to claim household items.

If you prepare any paperwork, send it to everyone at the same time. Keep careful records of who received what, and when that happened.

Keep your weekly reports going out to all of the beneficiaries. If you turn down a request from one beneficiary, turn down the same request if it comes from another beneficiary. Treat them all equally and make sure they all know you are doing this.

If one beneficiary asks for an advance on his or her inheritance, either turn down the request, or make an interim distribution to all of the beneficiaries at the same time; again, be sure not to overpay when doing an interim distribution because later on you need to deal with taxes and other expenses.

You should also be aware that the even-hand rule applies where there is a trust set up for one beneficiary, with the remains of the trust going to a second beneficiary on the death of the first. This is often seen in blended families where assets may be held in trust for the deceased's spouse, with the remainder of those assets going to the deceased's children on the death of the spouse. It is also seen in other situations.

For example, the deceased might leave his home and contents in trust so that his second wife may live in the home for the rest of her life. The terms of the trust might say that on the death of the second wife, the contents of the house are to be divided among the man's children from his first marriage. The house would be sold and the proceeds divided among his children.

The even-hand rule says that you have to be impartial between the first beneficiary (in this case, the spouse) and the second beneficiaries (the children). This is pretty tricky, especially if the trust is written so that you have discretion as to how much you are to pay or give to the spouse during his or her lifetime. Trusts are usually not written with a specific monthly or annual amount to be paid out; they generally leave that decision up to the executor.

You may find that the spouse is unhappy with the amount you are supplying from the trust, and that he or she may take you to court to force you to pay more. On the other hand, if you are too generous, you may upset the secondary beneficiaries (the children) who may complain that you are unfairly using up their inheritance.

If you must administer a will with a trust like this, read the wording of the will carefully. Lawyers have been aware of the even-hand rule for many years, and some have drafted their trusts with a specific mention of how the executor is to deal with the rule. Look for wording such as "my executor is not bound by the even-hand rule," which will certainly help to guide you in how you deal with the trust. It will also allow you to respond to beneficiaries who complain about your administration.

10
The Executor Must Finish the Estate in Reasonable Time

Taking too long to pay the beneficiaries and finish the estate is another of the more common complaints levelled against executors. This arises in part because beneficiaries do not really know how long it takes to wrap up an estate. Beneficiaries do not necessarily know what you are doing or what roadblocks you may have encountered. Many complaints such as "the executor is taking too long" or "the executor isn't doing anything" could be headed off with better communication with the beneficiaries.

The regular communication arrangement discussed in Chapter 4 will go a long way towards heading off this type of complaint against you. Educate the beneficiaries about the amount of work it takes to wrap up an estate. Regular communication will also make it clear to beneficiaries that sometimes the delay is not your fault. For example, if you have filed the probate application at the court and are waiting for it to arrive, any delays on that front are not within your control. The beneficiaries will assume that delays are your fault if you do not advise them otherwise.

1. The Executor's Year

You may have heard the term "the executor's year." This is a rule of thumb that is followed in Canada and applies to all executors and administrators. It means that an executor should be able to wrap up a simple estate in a year, unless of course there are lawsuits, claims, or other unusual complications that must be dealt with.

It does not mean that if a year passes by and you have not completed every single task in the estate, you will be unceremoniously dumped from your role as executor, or sued for negligence. It does mean that you have been given a time limit that you should use as your guideline. After the executor's year has elapsed, beneficiaries have the right to ask the court to hurry you along by whatever means the court feels is appropriate.

Realistically, even the simplest estate will require a year to complete, and most take longer. However, this rule of thumb will at least give you an idea of what is expected of you. It is not reasonable for a beneficiary to expect you to have everything finished in a month or two.

Is the estate you are working on a complicated estate? Should the beneficiaries expect you to wind up the estate within a year? Sometimes an estate looks relatively simple until the executor investigates more closely and finds more detail. An estate that has a valid will and contains a house, bank account, and RRIF to be divided among the children is not considered to be complicated. You should be able to wrap up an estate like that within a year.

Estates that are considered complex and therefore do not generally fall within the expectation of being finalized during the executor's year will usually include one or more of the following:

- A will that requires court interpretation due to unclear wording or incomplete instructions.

- A dispute over who will act as administrator where there is no will.

- A claim by a dependent for a greater share of the estate.

- A challenge to the will based on the grounds of undue influence or lack of testamentary capacity.

- A missing heir.

- A business owned by the deceased that must be sold or dissolved.

- Real estate owned by the deceased outside of Canada.

- A dispute about ownership of property, such as intergenerational joint property.

- A lawsuit against the deceased that was begun while the deceased was alive and must be concluded.

- A lawsuit against the executor.

Unexpected events frequently happen during the administration of an estate. Anything from the death of a beneficiary to the discovery of a tangled tax issue might arise and delay the completion of your role as executor. As mentioned earlier, keeping the beneficiaries informed of obstacles that arise and how you are meeting the challenges will help manage their expectations of your timeline.

2. The Court's Position

In 2013, the British Columbia court heard the case of *Reznik v. Matty*, a case that clarifies some important issues for executors. Mr. Matty died, leaving his son, Chad Matty, named as the executor. Chad and his three siblings were to share the estate equally. Chad made an interim distribution of $25,000 to each of the beneficiaries.

Chad did not distribute the rest of the estate, which amounted to more than $500,000, including a company, cash, and real estate. He refused to distribute the rest, despite the requests and demands of his siblings. Eventually the other three siblings took Chad to court, and asked the court to order Chad to distribute some of the estate. They asked for a further $20,000 each. By this time, Chad had been holding onto estate assets for an unbelievable 12 years.

Chad and his lawyer made some creative arguments to the court. One of Chad's arguments was that the court could remove Chad as executor if it wanted to, but could not order him to make a distribution. The court disagreed, and found that the higher court has the power to settle civil disputes, such as this dispute about the estate. Probate matters are heard in the superior, or higher, court in every province.

Another argument put forward by Chad was that there was a clause in the will that allowed him to decide when any asset was to be sold or cashed. The clause he referred to is one that is standard in most wills across Canada and therefore affects thousands of executors. It specifically allows an executor to "retain assets for such length of time as my Trustee shall deem advisable." Chad is not the first executor to attempt to rely on that clause as an excuse to take years to wind up an estate, nor will he be the last, but the court did not allow it.

The court said that this clause in the will did not displace the executor's overriding duty to settle the estate and distribute in a timely manner. This is important for executors to understand. The court will not allow you to take years to wrap up an estate simply because you believe the will's wording allows you to do that. The key phrase is "just cause." If there is no real reason not to distribute the estate, you must do so.

In this case, Chad did not give any reason for not distributing the estate, other than the fact that he did not want to and believed he could take as long as he wanted. The court ordered him to distribute $10,000 to each beneficiary immediately.

The court went on to say that an executor will not be forced to make a distribution on an estate where the estate assets are still needed for the payment of debts and expenses.

This case is an important decision for beneficiaries seeking a distribution where an executor unreasonably delays. On the other hand, it is important to keep in mind that in this case the executor was taking an unusually long time to administer the estate, and there were clearly sufficient assets to meet future expenses. The courts are likely to give executors a fair amount of leeway in determining the timing of distributions as long as they are acting reasonably.

What executors should learn from cases such as this one is that the courts will not simply sit back and allow executors to drag things on endlessly. Executors are expected to distribute the estate as soon as they are sure that they have enough funds on hand to pay the estate expenses and taxes. If an executor does not have a good reason for delaying, the beneficiaries who apply to the court for help are likely going to be successful.

This means that not only might you be forced to carry out the estate tasks before you wish to do so, but you may also be ordered to pay the costs of the beneficiaries' lawyer out of your own funds.

3. Interim Distribution

Throughout this book, you have been urged to take steps to protect yourself from liability by acting cautiously. In this chapter, however, the discussion has centered on the fact that you cannot delay the distribution of the estate without causing problems. These two points may seem contradictory, and you may well wonder how to achieve both goals.

One of the tools that is available to you is the interim distribution of the estate. While this is not something that an executor is legally required to do (other than in the case of undue delay), it is carried out in the vast majority of estates in Canada and beneficiaries may well request that you do the same.

An interim distribution refers to paying the beneficiaries the bulk of their inheritance while holding on to enough money in the estate to pay any taxes that may be owing and any final expenses. It differs from a final distribution in that it takes place before the executor has received a Tax Clearance Certificate from Canada Revenue Agency. (See Chapter 17 for more about how obtaining a Tax Clearance Certificate can help to protect you from liability.)

In law, an executor is required to ensure that all liabilities of the deceased and of the estate are paid before the estate is distributed to the beneficiaries. This includes taxes. The only way that an executor knows for sure that there are no more taxes owing by the deceased or the estate is to obtain a Tax Clearance Certificate. Therefore, in theory, an executor should never distribute an estate before receiving the certificate.

Unfortunately, obtaining the Tax Clearance Certificate can take months, and possibly a year after applying. There appears to be no way to speed up the process. Adding to the lengthy timeline is the fact that an executor cannot even apply for the certificate until the estate has been substantially finished. As we have seen in the previous section of this book, an executor can get into trouble for holding on to estate assets that are not needed for the payment of taxes and expenses.

The interim distribution developed as a way of making everyone happy. If doing interim distributions, the executor prepares a Statement of Proposed Distribution (see Sample 3) that clearly shows the beneficiaries that part of the estate is going to be held back until the clearance certificate arrives.

If you are contemplating an interim distribution, be careful about the amount that you decide to hold back. You are strongly urged to hire an accountant to estimate the tax that will be payable by the estate. It is very easy to make up an estimate of your own based on the deceased's previous years' liability, but this is generally not a good idea. During the estate administration, many assets are sold or cashed in. Some of these may have an impact on the deceased's final tax situation so that it no longer resembles earlier years.

Once you have figured out or are advised by the accountant as to how much tax is likely to be payable, allow yourself a reasonable margin of error, or "cushion," by inflating the amount a bit. This may be needed if there is unanticipated interest or penalties, or if there has been an error in the tax return.

Also consider any final expenses that you will incur once the certificate is received and you pay out the beneficiaries. There may be final legal fees or accounting fees to take into account. If you have not yet paid yourself your executor's fee, you should remember to allow for that to be paid. You may also have final out-of-pocket expenses. Add these final expenses to the amount you are holding back for taxes.

To illustrate how an interim distribution works, let us assume that Quint is the executor of an estate that currently has $346,998. He has gathered in all of the assets and paid all of the bills. His accountant has applied for the Tax Clearance Certificate and Quint knows it is going to be several months before he receives it. The three beneficiaries of the estate would prefer not to wait any longer to receive their shares, and they ask Quint to carry out an interim distribution.

Quint's accountant has told him that he should expect a tax bill of about $20,000. Quint has not yet been paid his executor's fee, which he calculates should be about $7,000. The accountant will be sending him one final bill after the certificate arrives, and Quint believes that bill will be in the range of $1,000. Altogether, he anticipates that he will need $28,000. Just to be on the safe side, he decides to hold back $40,000.

Quint's Statement of Proposed Distribution would look like Sample 3. (For more about Statements of Proposed Distribution, see Chapter 12.)

Sample 3
Statement of Proposed Distribution

The Estate of _____Roger Morrison_____, Deceased

Statement of Proposed Distribution

For the period from __Feb. 5, 2015__ to _____

FUNDS HELD IN THE ESTATE		$ 346,998.00
Holdback for taxes	$ 20,000.00	
Holdback for expenses	$ 7,000.00	
Executor's compensation	$ 13,000.00	
FUNDS AVAILABLE FOR DISTRIBUTION AFTER HOLDBACKS AND EXECUTOR'S COMPENSATION		$ 306,998.00
To be paid to beneficiary Anna	$ 102,332.67	
To be paid to beneficiary Rachel	$ 102,332.67	
To be paid to beneficiary Michael	$ 102,332.66	
FUNDS THEN REMAINING IN ESTATE		NONE

Quint would circulate this statement together with the rest of his accounting, and if the beneficiaries agree, he will send them their cheques. He will hold on to the $40,000 until he receives the Tax Clearance Certificate, at which time he will pay the taxes. He will also pay himself his executor's fee and pay the accountant. He will then divide any funds that are left over, equally among the three beneficiaries.

Normally, when an executor is distributing the bulk of the estate in an interim distribution, he will provide his full accounting to the beneficiaries at that time. He will also provide them with a release form to sign. If the final distribution is quite small, as it is in Sample 3, the executor normally would not go to the expense of preparing another full accounting. A brief statement showing how the remaining funds (in this case the $40,000) were spent should be sufficient.

Most estates do not have more than one interim distribution, but that is because most estates do not have complicated assets that take time to sell or transfer. If you are working on a complex estate in which one particular asset will not be sold for quite some time but other assets are already sold, you may decide to do an interim distribution now, followed by another when that major asset is sold. You have the discretion to decide that, though you are well advised to talk it over not just with the beneficiaries, but also with the estate accountant before going ahead.

The danger to the executor is in paying out a distribution without holding onto enough money to pay taxes. If you do that, you may not be able to recover any funds from the beneficiaries, as they are not legally required to refund any distributions. You may well end up paying for any shortfall out of your own personal funds.

11
The Executor Must Handle Lawsuits Properly

If you are fortunate, you will not have to handle a lawsuit on behalf of the estate. It is not something that happens to every executor, by any means. However, if you are required to look after legal matters for the estate, you can easily incur liability for dealing with them improperly. This chapter will look at three common errors that executors make.

The fact is that situations that could give rise to a lawsuit are almost endless. The suits may either be driven by the executor, brought by the beneficiaries, or instigated by a third party. In each case, the estate relies on the executor to speak and act on its behalf. Some of the potential lawsuits in which an executor may be involved are:

- A claim by a dependent such as a spouse, common-law spouse, disabled child, or other financial dependent for a larger share of the estate. There may be more than one person making competing claims against the estate. This type of claim was discussed in Chapter 8.

- A challenge to the validity of the will itself based on the alleged inability of the deceased to make a will. This lawsuit will be based on either or both of undue influence or lack of testamentary capacity. Undue influence refers to a situation in which a testator was forced, tricked, or persuaded to change his or her will in favour of someone else. Lack of testamentary capacity means that the testator did not have a full understanding of what he or she was doing at the time will instructions were given, or at the time the will was signed. These claims are brought by beneficiaries of the estate, or individuals who allege that they would be beneficiaries had the testator not been made to change the will.

- An application to the court for assistance in interpreting the will when wording is unclear or the executor needs help in taking the next step. This application would be started by the executor himself or herself. This type of application was discussed in Chapter 6 of this book.

- An application to the court to have an executor removed or to have other orders made to force the executor to carry on with the estate, as discussed in Chapter 13. These applications are brought by the beneficiaries.

- A dispute about assets that cannot be resolved by the beneficiaries or the executor. Examples would be a dispute over the ownership of joint assets, as was discussed in Chapter 8 of this book, or a dispute over who was intended by the deceased to inherit an asset with a designated beneficiary. These applications might be brought by either the executor or the beneficiaries.

- A challenge to the distribution of the estate by an individual who claims that he or she was promised something from the estate, and who had over the years contributed to the estate because he or she expected to inherit it. This type of claim is called constructive trust, or unjust enrichment, depending on the facts. The claims are brought by an individual who may or may not already be a beneficiary of the estate.

- A claim by a spouse or former spouse based on provincial matrimonial property division laws.

This is not an exhaustive list, as estates have a way of creating the most unusual litigation. However, this list contains the most common lawsuits you might encounter.

1. Not Prosecuting a Third Party in Time

Every potential lawsuit has a limitation period, that is, a date by which the lawsuit must be started. If it is not begun on time, it can never be brought at all. This is not just applicable to estates; it is applicable to all lawsuits in civil court. If you, as executor, were to miss a deadline and that mistake resulted in the estate not receiving some benefit it would otherwise have received, you will be liable for that loss personally.

Pay particular attention to any debts owed to the estate. As an executor, you are obligated to collect any money or other assets owed to the deceased or to the estate. Get started on collecting those debts as soon as possible, so that if your initial requests or attempts should fail, you will have time to begin a lawsuit on time.

Another potential lawsuit that you should be aware of will arise if the deceased passed away as a result of an accident or some action by another person or company. You may be required to sue the individual or organization for wrongful death, negligence, or other action depending on the facts of the situation. Some of the possible lawsuits would be:

- A claim against the driver and/or owner of a vehicle that collided with and killed the deceased.

- A claim against the manufacturer of a product that did not work properly and killed the deceased.

- A claim against a person, company, or municipality that failed to warn the public about a dangerous situation, and which resulted in the death of the deceased.

- A claim against the owner of an animal that killed the deceased.

- A claim against a business whose operations, equipment, or policies did not meet safety standards and resulted in the death of the deceased.

- A claim against a doctor or nursing home who failed to provide proper medical care.

As you can see, the possibilities are almost endless. If the deceased was killed directly or indirectly by the actions of another, you should consider your obligation to sue on behalf of the deceased.

Most lawsuits have a limitation period of two years from the date of the incident. However, this limitation period may vary. For example, if you are required to sue a municipality, you may find that the deadline is shorter than two years. Do not assume that you know how long the limitation period is, or that you know exactly when it began. Always consult a litigation lawyer to talk about limitation periods.

Litigation on estates has unusual challenges when it comes to limitations. As we have seen in several examples in this book, the legislation regarding estates often simply refers to "reasonable time" for someone to take certain steps.

1.1 Unreasonable prosecution on behalf of the estate

Whenever an executor brings a lawsuit on behalf of the estate, or continues one, he or she is said to be prosecuting that lawsuit. This word contrasts with the situation where the executor has no choice but to defend the estate against a lawsuit brought by others.

Chapter 6, section **4.** discussed the need for both executors and beneficiaries to be reasonable when starting lawsuits, and when continuing lawsuits. Continuing a lawsuit in this context means:

- To refuse to withdraw your claim even when you can see that the evidence against you is correct and overwhelming.

- To refuse to discuss settlement because you would rather fight it out until the end.

- To refuse to attend mediation even though that might quickly end the dispute.

- To appeal to higher courts even though there is really no legal reason for doing so.

- To take personal satisfaction in making the other party waste his or her time and money on court action even though you are not making any progress towards winning the case.

Estate litigation is unlike most other kinds of lawsuits. The people against whom you are fighting are usually family members. The issues in dispute can be very sensitive ones, such as an argument over whether a sibling took advantage of an aging parent. If you are both executor and family member, it will be extremely difficult to keep your objectivity. It will be tempting to vent your anger or frustration on other people, such as the person on the other side of the legal dispute. You may really want to hurt or punish them, in a way that would simply not arise if the lawsuit were against strangers.

Try to remember that giving in to that anger is only going to make things worse for you. Not only will you lose the lawsuit, but you will then likely be reprimanded by the judge and ordered to pay the legal bills for both sides.

2. Improper Settlements

One of the ways in which an executor can make an improper settlement on behalf of an estate is to fail to investigate a claim against the estate before agreeing on a settlement. As an executor, you are responsible for safeguarding all estate assets. If you pay out funds to someone to whom they were not really owed, you are causing a financial loss to the estate.

You may or may not choose to advertise for creditors and claimants, as described in Chapter 17 of this book. Regardless of whether a claim comes to your attention through such an advertisement, you have a duty to check it out as best you can. At the very least, request paperwork such as work orders, contracts, or promissory notes to back up the request that the claimant has presented.

Once you know the facts of the claim, go through the deceased's paperwork to see if you can find anything pertaining to the claim. Look for cancelled cheques or receipts for payment. Look for a copy of the paperwork marked "paid." You should also check into whether the claim being made has a limitation date that would bar the claimant from collecting from the estate.

Another way in which an executor can improperly settle a claim is to neglect to collect money that is owing to the estate. To be fair, sometimes an executor will choose not to collect a sum that is smaller than the sum required to do the collection. An example would be a subscription to a magazine where it would cost more for you to contact its office and cancel the subscription than would be received as a refund.

Ideally, the will you are administering will contain a clause that specifically allows you to decide whether or not to collect these small claims. If it does not, make sure you protect yourself by printing a letter or an email from the debtor that shows what it would cost to collect it.

A third way in which an executor can run afoul of the responsibility to the estate is to settle a claim against the estate for an unreasonably small amount. The opportunity to settle matters will often present itself during estate litigation, as it is usually cheaper and less stressful for parties to negotiate a settlement than it is to take the matter all the way through the courts. The dispute that led to the claim may be driven by beneficiaries of the estate, or by third parties.

Resist the temptation to make a foolish settlement simply to put an end to the matter. While the desire to reach a settlement is an admirable one, you cannot allow the estate to be depleted by a claim simply because you lack the energy to defend it. You should consult a lawyer, unless the claim is too small to justify doing so. If the claim is large and it appears that the estate and the claimant are very far apart on a potential settlement, consider going to mediation. While you must be willing to reach a settlement where one is possible, you have an obligation to reach the most advantageous settlement that you can.

If the claim in question is with someone other than the residuary beneficiaries, you might consider talking over a possible settlement with them before accepting it. If you have their approval of the settlement you wish to make, you are much less likely to run into objections from them later on.

Make sure that you keep all paperwork, including printouts of email messages, that pertain to the claim and the settlement. If you are challenged by the beneficiaries on the settlement amount, you will need to be able to show the steps you took to reach an agreement. Once you reach an agreement with any claimant, request a signed release that includes a bar to any future pursuit of the claim by the claimant.

Release form requirements may vary by province or territory. You could ask a lawyer to draft a release form for you to use, or check with your provincial probate registry as some registries offer fillable release forms online.

12

The Executor Must Provide a Proper Accounting

Given the number of disputes and lawsuits that arise from executors' accountings, the task of preparing an accounting seems to be one that stymies most executors. This chapter will provide you with information and ideas that will help you prepare an accurate, thorough accounting to the beneficiaries.

In the *Gibbons Estate* (Alberta, 2009), the executor could not seem to provide an accounting that satisfied the beneficiaries. Whether the executor was unable to produce a proper accounting, or was simply unwilling to do so, was not clear. The beneficiaries requested an accounting several times over a number of years, without receiving one. When they finally did receive one, they found it confusing and full of holes. They could not get answers from the executor.

The beneficiaries hired a lawyer, who corresponded with the executor in an attempt with requests to clarify outstanding accounting matters. Specific questions were asked. The executor did not comply. The answers were either not provided, or were even more confusing than the original material. Eventually the beneficiaries asked the court for help.

The court ordered the executor more than once to come up with a better accounting, but still he did not. Eventually the beneficiaries were forced to conclude that the executor's refusal to provide details was an attempt to hide the fact that estate funds were missing. The matter went back and forth between the executor and the beneficiaries. The executor wanted the beneficiaries to approve his accounting, but the beneficiaries believed there was something missing. Eventually the executor asked the court to pass his accounts, saying that the beneficiaries were being unreasonable and could never be satisfied.

The judge was strict with the executor, saying that the executor had had plenty of time and opportunity to fulfill his duty to provide a decent accounting. As a result, the judge ordered the following:

- The executor was removed from the job of executor.

- Any money that was not properly accounted for in the executor's accounting, as well as interest on that money, was to be deducted from the executor's fee.

- Any expense for which there was not a satisfactory explanation was also to be deducted from the executor's fee.

- The cost of the beneficiaries' lawyers for all of the court applications were to be paid by the executor. He also had to pay his own lawyer as this was not to be covered by the estate.

- The executor was allowed an executor's fee of $15,558, but the deductions and penalties against him were set at $158,321, meaning that not only was his fee eaten up but he was left with an enormous debt to pay back to the estate.

- As the executor was also a beneficiary of the estate, any inheritance he would otherwise have received was used to pay off some of this cost.

The executor appealed the decision to the higher court, but was not successful.

Applications in court between executors wanting their accounts to be passed and beneficiaries wanting a better accounting are commonplace. The impetus for the court application can come from either the executor or the beneficiaries, depending on the situation. What can be learned from cases such as the Gibbons estate described above is that the courts will insist that executors do the job they agreed to do by becoming executors in the first place. Failure to provide a thorough accounting within a reasonable time is considered to be a breach of the fiduciary duty that an executor owes to the estate.

You should understand how important it is to account for all of the funds that you have handled as executor. Beneficiaries know that they can ask the court to force you to account, and the courts have made it clear that they will crack down on executors who refuse to account properly.

The three documents that compose the main components of your accounting are:

1. Statement of Receipts and Disbursements.

2. Statement of Proposed Executor's Compensation.

3. Statement of Proposed Distribution.

There are almost no forms prescribed by the provincial or territorial governments for an executor's accounting. Even where forms are prescribed, it is extremely rare that an accounting that is otherwise complete, accurate, and understandable would be rejected due to improper form. Using the documents suggested in this book, all of which are described in some detail below, will allow you to present all of the information the beneficiaries require. It is up to you to ensure that you enter all of the transactions correctly.

The download kit that accompanies this book contains samples of each of these documents for you to use as templates for your own accounting. If you have prepared an accounting using some other format, compare it with these documents to see whether you have in fact included all of the necessary components. If so, you need not change your current format.

1. Statement of Receipts and Disbursements

In Chapter 7 of this book, we discussed setting up a ledger to keep track of all of the transactions you handle on behalf of the estate. If you have been keeping a ledger like that, you will find that you can quickly and easily convert the ledger into a Statement of Receipts and Disbursements. To convert the ledger, follow these steps:

1. Total all of the funds received and enter that total at the bottom of the "Received" column.

2. Do the same for the "Paid" column.

3. Clearly describe these numbers as totals so that they are not mistaken for ledger entries.

4. Check to ensure that the total of the received funds minus the total of the paid funds equals the amount shown in the "Balance" column. If it does not, you have an error somewhere in

your calculations. Check your math and your original entries until you are able to make the statement balance.

5. At the top of the statement, insert the dates to indicate the time period that is covered by your statement. Typically, the starting date is the day after the deceased died, even if you might not have any entries right away. The closing date is the date of the last transaction on your statement. The dates become very important if you are making an interim distribution, or if you are asking beneficiaries to sign a Release.

Sample 4 shows how your Statement of Receipts and Disbursements should look. Yours is likely to be quite a bit lengthier than this example.

Sample 4
Statement of Receipts and Disbursements

The Estate of _____Roger Morrison_____, Deceased

Executor's Statement of Receipts and Disbursements

For the period from __Feb. 5, 2015__ to __June 30, 2015__

Date	Received	Paid	Details
2014-02-23	2,500.00	0.00	Received CPP death benefit
2014-02-26	17,891.27	0.00	Cashed in TD account #12345
2014-02-27	0.00	9,875.33	Paid funeral
2014-05-31	398,000.00	0.00	Proceeds of sale of house
2014-06-14	0.00	1,025.69	Paid Visa card
2014-06-22	0.00	450.00	Paid ambulance bill
Total:	418,391.27	11,351.02	Balance of funds in the estate = $407,040.25

2. Statement of Proposed Executor's Compensation

In the Statement of Proposed Executor's Compensation, you are advising the beneficiaries of the amount you wish to be paid for your work on the estate. The amount you request will be a combination of wages and reimbursement of out-of-pocket expenses. You will find more specific information as to the allowable amounts and expenses in sections **4.** and **5.**

The download kit accompanying this book contains a blank sample Statement of Proposed Executor's Compensation that you may use. You will note that it separates wages from expenses for the information of the beneficiaries, then provides one total.

In presenting the amount that you are claiming as a wage to compensate you for your work on the estate, you may break down the dollar amount into individual hours worked. This is not required, but sometimes executors who are expecting some resistance from the beneficiaries like to make it clear just how much work was actually required. Remember that you are not just being compensated for the number of hours you devoted to the estate; you are also being compensated for the risk you assumed when you took on the role of executor, as well as the inconvenience and stress of the role.

Whether or not you break the amount down into hours worked, you should always express the amount as a percentage of the gross estate. While a simply stated dollar amount may seem quite high to the beneficiaries, seeing it expressed as a percentage gives them more perspective. Calculating the percentage also requires you to consider whether the amount you are claiming is too high or too low.

The numbers used in Sample 5 are based on the fictitious estate you saw in section **1**.

3. Statement of Proposed Distribution

In the Statement of Proposed Distribution, you are showing the beneficiaries how you propose to divide the estate. This statement will use the numbers you came up with when you prepared your Statement of Proposed Executor's Compensation and your Statement of Receipts and Disbursements, so do those first before you attempt to calculate the distribution.

The download kit accompanying this book contains a blank sample Statement of Proposed Distribution that you may use. It is applicable whether you are making an interim or a final distribution.

The idea behind this statement is to start off with the amount that is currently in the estate, per your Statement of Receipts and Disbursements, then subtract an amount that is being held back to cover taxes, final expenses and your executor's compensation. Subtracting those holdbacks will leave a net amount, which you will divide according to the will. If you are an administrator, the net amount is divided according to local intestacy law.

If you are preparing a final distribution, the final line of the statement should always indicate that there are no funds remaining in

Sample 5
Statement of Proposed Executor's Compensation

The Estate of _____Roger Morrison_____, Deceased

Statement of Proposed Executor's Compensation

Date _July 31, 2015_

1. Wages		
I am claiming 200 hours @ $20 per hour = $4,000.00 This represents less that 1% of the estate (1% x 418,391.27 = 4,183.91)	$ 4,000.00	
Subtotal A	$ 4,000.00	$ 4,000.00
2. Expenses		
I am claiming $198.57 in out-of-pocket expenses	$ 198.57	
I am also claiming 212 kilometres driven @ 0.39 per km	$ 82.68	
Subtotal B	$ 281.25	$ 281.25
Total A + B		$ 4,281.25

the estate. If you are preparing an interim distribution, your last line should also indicate that there are no funds remaining, but you will have reserved some funds in the holdback section. If any of the funds that have been held back are left over once expenses and taxes have been paid, those funds must be distributed to the beneficiaries.

A sample Statement of Proposed Distribution has been prepared in Sample 6, using the Statement of Receipts and Disbursements from section **1.** and the Statement of Proposed Executor's Compensation from section **2.** of this chapter.

Note that for the first line of the Statement of Proposed Distribution, you use the final number, or the "funds remaining in the estate" from the last page of your Statement of Receipts and Disbursements.

4. How to Calculate Your Compensation

The amount of executor's compensation is a problem on a large proportion of estates. This is partly because the amount taken by an executor as his or her honorarium reduces the amount left in the estate to be divided up among the beneficiaries. Knowing that the funds

Sample 6
Statement of Proposed Distribution

The Estate of ___Roger Morrison___ , Deceased

Statement of Proposed Distribution

Date _July 31, 2015_

FUNDS HELD IN THE ESTATE		$ 407,040.25
Holdback for taxes	$ 10,000.00	
Holdback for expenses	$ 5,000.00	
Executor's compensation	$ 4,281.25	
FUNDS AVAILABLE FOR DISTRIBUTION AFTER HOLDBACKS AND EXECUTOR'S COMPENSATION		$ 387,759.00
To be paid to beneficiary A	$ 129,253.00	
To be paid to beneficiary B	$ 129,253.00	
To be paid to beneficiary C	$ 129,253.00	
FUNDS THEN REMAINING IN ESTATE		NONE

come directly out of their pockets, beneficiaries are usually vigilant about the amount allowed.

Executors are also part of the problem. There is a range of fees available to an executor for his or her work. The accepted scale in Canada is between 1 and 5 percent of an estate. The scale exists rather than a universal flat fee because some estates are more complicated than others due to complex family arrangements or assets. Having a range of fees available is intended to ensure that the executor who must deal with selling a home in the USA, or finding and paying beneficiaries in Europe, or winding down the deceased's business will be paid more than the executor who simply cashes in one investment account.

The problem is that many executors go straight to the 5 percent and claim the maximum whether their work justifies that amount or not. Their feeling is that if it is available, they should take it, ignoring the fact that the maximum payment is not fitting. In some cases, the amount of fighting and backstabbing among families makes the estate so difficult and time-consuming that an executor might feel entitled to a higher payment (and might get one, for that matter). In plenty of cases, though, the executor is simply being greedy. Anyone with a grain of sense should be able to see that a beneficiary will object to an executor who does minimal work collecting maximum pay. You will avoid many disputes by simply keeping your expectations reasonable.

Determining how much compensation you should claim is more complicated than simply deciding that you want the most that you can get. There is a process to the decision. First, check the will for any statement about how much you should be paid. Unfortunately, most wills do not say anything about it, but that is changing as lawyers and clients alike learn from the ongoing estate litigation in Canada. If the will does set an amount or a percentage, it is the maximum you may claim. If the will says you get 2 per cent for taking care of the estate, then you get 2 per cent and the court will not allow anything higher.

If you are named as the executor of a will which sets your potential payment at an amount that is too low for you to accept, or perhaps states that you are not to be paid at all, your only real option is to turn down the job right from the start. Once you begin working on the estate, you are bound by the terms of the will. This fee, of course, does not cover unanticipated situations such as a lawsuit that you have to deal with on behalf of the estate.

If the will does not say anything about the amount of compensation you are allowed to claim, you must fall back on the amounts allowed by provincial or territorial statutes, and the common-law body of case law in which judges have set compensation in other estates. This is where the standard of 1 to 5 per cent developed.

Your best bet is to keep good records of the work you do on the estate so that you may define your work in terms of how many hours you put in, and the kind of work you did during those hours. There are other considerations, though. Other factors that you should consider when deciding on your fee include:

- Whether there was an outright distribution of the estate, or whether you have had to manage trusts for beneficiaries. The responsibility of looking after invested funds and disbursing them appropriately merits a higher fee than simply transferring the same amount of money to someone in one single payment.

- The value of the estate. A larger estate means that you as an executor carry more risk.

- Whether your work has involved many individual transactions, such as various bank accounts, numerous bills to be paid, or an unusually large number of beneficiaries. Note that five or six beneficiaries do not constitute an "unusually large" number. This usually refers to a situation in which there are a dozen or more individual beneficiaries.

- The complexity of the work involved. In some estates, the executor has to work with shareholders' agreements, tax specialists, or government agencies. The more complex estates warrant a higher fee.

- Whether any difficult or unusual questions were raised. This might mean that you have had to ask the court for advice, such as the interpretation of wording in the will, or guidance on trust terms.

- The amount of skill, labour, responsibility, technological support, and specialized knowledge required. This could come into play if you had to deal with an estate that involved a large number of digital assets, a collection of rare musical instruments, or royalties on tangible art sales in foreign countries.

- The number and complexity of tasks delegated to others. The more you have delegated to others, the smaller your fee should be.

- The number of executors or administrators. If there is more than one, you must share the fee between you. Between the two of you, the total fee may not exceed the maximum.

There is no exact formula or recipe for mixing together all of these factors and coming up with a percentage that is appropriate. However, you should be able to tell by examining this list of factors whether you should in fact be claiming the maximum amount of executor's compensation. Do not forget that the beneficiaries have access to this knowledge too, and will also be aware if you have not earned the maximum amount of pay.

There are some circumstances in which an executor may claim compensation that is greater than the 5 per cent normally considered to be the maximum fee. They are rare, but if you find yourself in one of these situations, you are entitled to additional compensation. Generally, those circumstances would include:

- Being called on to perform additional roles in order to administer the estate, such as having to manage a business owned by the deceased.

- Having to act as a director of a corporation, as this role by its very nature brings increased legal risk to you.

- Encountering unusual difficulties or situations. This could be anything from having to evict unwilling tenants to dealing with beneficiaries who assault each other.

- Having to deal with litigation against the estate or on behalf of the estate.

An important detail that causes trouble if overlooked is the fact that when there are two or more executors administering an estate, the fee is split among them. They do not each get the full percentage. If the will says the executor is to get 2 per cent and names two co-executors, then each of them gets 1 per cent, unless they agree on a different split.

Note that you are entitled to charge for out-of-pocket expenses over and above your fee. See the next section of this book for detailed information about which expenses you may claim.

Once you have determined the amount that you wish to claim as compensation, you will prepare your executor's accounting as described earlier in this chapter. You will include a statement in the accounting that shows what you want to claim, and how you arrived at that fee. Make sure that it is expressed as a percentage of the estate as well as a dollar amount. This is part of the documentation that goes to the beneficiaries at the end of the estate when you are ready to pay them their inheritance.

If the beneficiaries agree to the amount that you have claimed as your fee, then you may pay that to yourself from the estate. Normally the agreement of the beneficiaries is given in writing in the form of a Release that approves of all of the executor's accounts. At this point, some executors go off the rails and lose their tempers as they do not see why the beneficiaries get to approve or veto their fees. Keep in mind that the beneficiaries are entitled by law to inherit "the rest of" the estate, and your fee comes out of that fund. This gives them the right to oversee your compensation and your expenses.

5. Which Expenses You May Claim

Expenses claimed by executors frequently lead to disputes on estates. Some executors take the approach that everything they pay out should be reimbursed by the estate, but this is simply not the case.

Typically an executor will fly in from out of town to attend the funeral. He or she will stay in a hotel with the rest of his or her family, then in a day or two go back home. The next thing the beneficiaries know, the executor has repaid himself for the flights, the hotels, the meals, the rental car, and in some cases even clothing to wear to the funeral. None of these is an acceptable expense and you should not claim any of them.

You are not coming to the funeral because you are the executor. The executor's presence is not required by law. You are attending because you are a family member or friend. Everyone pays his or her own way to a funeral and you are no exception. As for your family, none of them are executors in any event so none of their expenses should ever be covered by the estate.

If that same executor who flew in for a few days also took the time to work on the estate while in town, that is a different story. Perhaps the executor located the original will, met with family members to talk about distribution of personal items, changed the locks on the house and found a home for the deceased's pet. In that case, the executor could charge expenses for the trip. However, if the executor did only a couple of hours of work on the estate, it is excessive to charge for a week in a hotel.

The law allows an executor to take reasonable expenses that are incurred in administering the estate. Attempts to push that past reasonable and into excessive are almost guaranteed to start a quarrel with the beneficiaries. You must be conservative and use common sense.

Make sure you keep all receipts and invoices for expenses. Also ensure that you keep track of your mileage, as you are entitled to be reimbursed for the driving you put in while looking after the estate.

6. How and When to Pay Yourself

Executors also cause problems for themselves by mismanaging the timing of their compensation payment to themselves. It is not a monthly paycheque. It is not intended to be a salary for you to live on. The compensation payment should be made only at the end of the estate administration when all bills and taxes are paid, and you are ready to pay the beneficiaries. If you take compensation before the end of the estate administration, it is referred to as "pre-taking," because it is premature.

If you pay yourself from the estate and are taken to court for a passing of accounts, you may be required to repay some or all of the compensation you have taken. The law doesn't allow for pre-taking compensation unless it is specifically stated in the will.

When the estate is ready to be finalized and you are ready to pay out the beneficiaries, you will produce an accounting that shows what you have done with all of the assets and liabilities of the estate. Your accounting explains to the beneficiaries what has happened with the assets, but it also tells the story of how much work you did and the issues you had to deal with along the way.

Part of the accounting package that you provide to the beneficiaries should contain a Statement of Proposed Executor's Compensation, as described earlier in this chapter. This document will set out exactly what fee you want to claim and exactly which expenses you claim for reimbursement. If an estate is rather small, some executors do not complete a separate document, but simply state an amount with no real explanation of how it was determined.

If the beneficiaries do not mind not seeing any calculations or explanations, you need not provide them. However, the vast majority of beneficiaries will insist on their right to full disclosure.

Another part of the same accounting package is the beneficiary release form. When a beneficiary signs the release, he or she is stating that he or she agrees with what you have done with the estate and agrees not to ever try to sue you or collect from you. Included in the release is a sentence that says the beneficiary agrees to the amount you have requested on your Statement of Proposed Executor's Compensation.

If the beneficiaries do not agree to the amount that you wish to claim, it is a good idea to negotiate with them to reach agreement. Perhaps they need to know more about what you did for the estate to appreciate the value of your work. On the other hand, perhaps you really are overcharging. If you and the beneficiaries are not able to agree, your last resort is to ask the court to pass your accounts and set your fee.

13
What Factors Are Considered by the Courts When Reviewing Cases

In each case brought before the courts by beneficiaries, the courts look at a number of factors when deciding whether or not an executor is liable for an error. These factors influence which of the possible steps that may be taken against an executor are appropriate in that case. The judge will examine the probate documents and any other relevant paperwork, but will also hear evidence from the beneficiaries and from the executor. There may be others whose evidence is heard as well. In other words, errors made by executors are looked at on a case-by-case basis.

In this chapter, we will examine the factors which a court will consider relevant in most cases. As estates vary widely from each other in terms of facts, dollar amounts, and the individuals involved, so will the treatment given to each case by the courts. The factors presented here are not necessarily presented in the order of priority given by a court and this is not an exhaustive list, rather simply the most common examples.

1. Size and Impact of the Error

Obviously a bigger mistake that cost the estate thousands of dollars is going to have more impact on the beneficiaries than a smaller mistake. A judge is going to find that depriving a beneficiary of $500,000 is more serious than depriving that same beneficiary of $500. While the breach by the executor might be the same, the impact on the beneficiary is much greater.

Part of the problem with a big mistake is that it may be impossible for the executor to repay the funds if it is a very large sum, so the beneficiaries might never recover what they have lost. Therefore the impact is greater because restitution cannot be made.

2. Personal Benefit by the Executor

When a mistake or oversight made by the executor is something that benefits the executor personally, it is harder for the executor to credibly say that it was an innocent error. This is particularly true if it went on for some time. Executors frequently delay the distribution of an estate when they are receiving funds or other benefits from that estate. For example, an executor who has always wanted to farm his or her father's land may simply decide not to transfer the title to the farm because he or she is making a good living by farming it.

This type of executor will have a harder time giving credible evidence that the mistake of not distributing the estate was simply an error.

Another mistake along these lines is made when an executor takes money out of a trust that is supposed to be held for children or other beneficiaries. When it is discovered that the funds were used to buy luxury goods or exotic vacations for the executor, it will result in more severe remedies by the courts than a situation in which the executor lost money due to poor investment strategy.

When an executor allows a member of his or her immediate family to gain some unfair benefit from the estate, such as living in the deceased's home without paying rent or driving the deceased's vehicle, this is also considered to be a personal benefit to the executor.

3. Good Faith

Good faith is a legal term that means a person is acting honestly and to the best of his or her ability with the information available to him or her. As a general rule, an executor who always acts in good faith will not face the same legal consequences as one who acts maliciously or negligently. Certainly, even honest executors can make mistakes, but the fact that one made an error in good faith rather than in his or her own self-interest is a major difference.

The good-faith standard must apply to each and every step you take as an executor. Proving that you acted in good faith may be somewhat difficult. As you can imagine, every executor who ever got into trouble tried to say that he or she was acting in good faith. The judge has heard it all before. However, if you follow the record-keeping tips and other suggestions in this book, you will be in a much stronger position. You will have copies of correspondence or emails in which you hired professionals and followed their advice. You will have appraisals to back up the selling price of assets. You will have evidence of your efforts to do your job properly.

Losses to an estate may occur with estate investments. When a court is determining the extent of an executor's liability with respect to investment losses, it will take into account any factors that are beyond the control of the executor. For example, the executor cannot be held responsible for inflation or poor economic conditions in general.

However, the court will also look at whether the executor obtained professional investment advice, and of course, whether that advice was actually followed. An executor who holds investments for an estate for any length of time would be wise to hire a professional financial advisor. They should get a written financial plan put into place that indicates factors such as how long the funds are to be invested, any tax planning steps taken, and how the balance of particular investments was achieved.

If the estate funds are invested for a long time, as would be the case with a trust for a beneficiary, it is also a good idea to interact with the financial advisor on a regular basis to keep an eye on what is happening with the funds. An annual meeting is probably enough to ensure that you are able to judge the results of the investments and to address any issues that may arise.

A clause that is very popular in wills these days is a clause that says as long as the executor is acting in good faith, he or she cannot be held liable for any mistakes. On the face of it, that clause would seem to give executors an awful lot of protection, but as mentioned, the executor must be able to demonstrate that he or she was acting in good faith.

4. Overall Conduct

If an executor's behaviour has been exemplary in every other aspect, a mistake may appear as nothing more than a simple accident. If the executor provides the judge with accurate, complete financial records and has evidence that he or she took every step properly, the judge may take the position that the executor is human and simply erred. This does not mean there will be no consequences for a loss caused by the executor, but it does mean that there may not be any punishment for the executor, nor is the executor likely to be removed from his or her role.

On the other hand, an executor who has refused to co-operate or communicate with anyone, who cannot show what he or she has done with estate funds, or perhaps cannot explain why the estate is taking so long to wrap up, may not meet with any sympathy at all. The court is the last resort for parties who are unable to resolve matters between them. If an executor forces the beneficiaries to use the courts through a hostile or arrogant attitude, the judge will not be happy to see him or her.

5. The Beneficiaries' Petition

Another factor that will feed into the decision of the court about what to do is the application made by the beneficiary. In his or her application, the beneficiary will ask for what he or she thinks is the right outcome.

As mentioned, most beneficiaries come right out and ask that the executor be removed from his or her duties. Usually an application against an executor will ask for several remedies as opposed to just one. For example, the beneficiary might ask that you be removed, but if the judge is not willing to do that, then as an alternative, the beneficiaries ask that deadlines be imposed.

This is not to say that a beneficiary will always get what he or she wants when asking for sanctions against you. Far from it! Judges are well aware of the dynamics of families and the volatility of estate litigation. The beneficiaries' request is a factor because a beneficiary will likely be prepared to bolster up a request for a certain action. For example, a beneficiary who petitions to have you removed from an estate is probably going to have someone else lined up to take your place. A judge is far more likely to remove you and appoint a neutral third party, than to remove you leaving nobody in charge. In this way, the beneficiary increases the chance that his or her request will be granted.

6. Beneficiary Acquiescence

"Beneficiary acquiescence" is the term used when a beneficiary knew of and possibly approved of the actions being taken by the executor but did not object to the actions at the time. As a general rule, the knowledge and approval of the beneficiaries will preclude them from later coming back and suing an executor for his or her actions. It is not a guarantee, but it is one of the strongest defences available to an executor.

This is the basic principle behind the practice of asking beneficiaries to sign a release document once the beneficiary has examined the executor's accounting. Once the beneficiary has signed the release, he or she cannot claim that the executor's steps were taken without his or her knowledge or approval. This also illustrates why beneficiaries may be reluctant to sign releases when they have not received a full accounting; they do not wish to give approval when they do not have all the facts.

There may be times when the beneficiaries of the estate you are administering will ask you to carry out a distribution that does not strictly follow the will. For example, the beneficiaries might all agree that it would be nice if the estate made a donation to a charity or hospital that had been extremely important to the deceased. If the will did not direct you to make this donation, doing so would cause you to breach your duty to distribute the estate according to the will.

This does not mean that the donation cannot be made. However, you should protect yourself by having all of the beneficiaries agree in writing that the change to the distribution has their approval. A verbal agreement is not sufficient. If you have that written agreement, a beneficiary who later decides that he or she is not happy that his or her inheritance was reduced by the amount of the donation cannot blame you for making the donation.

Another common example of beneficiary acquiescence is a beneficiary's wish to purchase a headstone for the deceased's grave. A headstone is not considered in law to be a necessary part of a burial or cremation, and therefore there is some argument about whether it is a true funeral expense. You may find, after spending the money on the headstone, that one or more beneficiaries object to the purchase. If you or the beneficiaries want to place a headstone, it would be a good idea to have all beneficiaries agree to its purchase in advance.

The above are examples of how beneficiaries and executors can work together to ensure that an executor is not held liable for actions that would otherwise be considered a breach of duty. However, the executor may also be able to rely on the acquiescence of the beneficiaries in matters that are in dispute and being heard by the courts. In other words, the beneficiary might not admit that he or she knew and approved of the executor's actions, but the court might still conclude that the knowledge and approval were there.

If a beneficiary hears about or suspects a breach of duty by the executor but does not object, this may well be construed as beneficiary acquiescence. The beneficiary must object to the actions within a reasonable time. Like most other rules regarding estates, there is no definition of reasonable time that fits every estate. Each case has different circumstances, so common sense must be used to determine what is reasonable.

Whether or not beneficiary acquiescence is applicable in any particular case, and whether or not it excuses the executor's actions, are matters that would have to be decided by the court.

14

Possible Consequences for an Executor Who Makes a Mistake on an Estate

There are many ways in which you, in your role as executor, may be held accountable for your work (or lack of it) on an estate. Once someone has died and you step in to look after the estate, you are on the hook immediately. Every step you take may be scrutinized by the beneficiaries of the estate, by creditors of the deceased, by Canada Revenue Agency, by the accountants who prepare estate tax returns, and by a judge, if it goes that far.

Most of the lawsuits against executors are brought by the beneficiaries. They are the ones who have a personal interest in the estate, and to whom the executor or administrator owes a fiduciary duty. Whether beneficiaries are individual people or charitable organizations, they can and should watch over what you are doing, and they will likely be the main source of complaints and friction. Depending on the facts, you might also run into trouble with the accountant or financial advisor, or Canada Revenue Agency.

Just as there is a range of errors, there is a range of responses available from the courts. In this chapter, you will find some of the orders a court might make against you if you are brought to the court by a dissatisfied party, starting with the least punitive and working our way up.

Although these responses, which in law are referred to as remedies, are listed and discussed individually, you should be aware that a court will combine as many of these remedies together as it sees fit. Some Canadian court cases are discussed throughout this book so that you may see how a judge may combine various remedies to suit a situation.

All of the possible remedies discussed in this chapter involve the courts. The very fact that an estate has to go through a lawsuit means that the estate is being placed in a situation that is less than ideal. Much of the time (but not always), your legal fees as an executor will be paid from the estate. This means there are fewer assets left in the estate to be distributed among the beneficiaries. It also means that there are delays while documents are filed and the scheduled court date rolls around.

For the executor, even one who may be blameless but needs to prove it, a lawsuit brings the stress of dealing with a high-pressure, unpleasant situation. It also means time away from work to prepare your case and appear in court. It may result in financial loss to you personally.

The real toll, however, is the damage done to family relationships when communication breaks down so badly that nothing can be resolved without resorting to the courts.

Your goal as an executor or administrator should be to conduct yourself and the estate in such a way as to avoid causing the beneficiaries to believe that they must make you accountable in court. However, no matter how reasonable and above-board you may be, there is no guarantee that the beneficiaries will also be reasonable. You may end up in court through no fault of your own.

In this chapter we will look at the possible consequences to an executor if mistakes are made on the estate.

1. Court-Imposed Deadlines

As you read earlier, beneficiaries will expect you to wrap up the estate in reasonable time. A judge might place deadlines on you if you are taking too long to carry out your estate duties. The deadline imposed will be a response to the facts alleged by the beneficiaries. It is not enough for them to arrive in court and announce that they are fed up with waiting for their money. They will have to be specific about tasks you have supposedly delayed.

For example, the judge might order you to put the deceased's house on the market within 30 days if you are taking too long to list it, or if you are allowing a family member to live there without paying rent. Or, the judge may require you to file a certain document within a certain number of days. This could be anything from an accounting to an affidavit.

If the judge imposes deadlines on you, this indicates that the judge still thinks you can do the executor's job, but that you are not being fair to the beneficiaries by dragging your feet.

2. Requirement to Account to Beneficiaries

A judge might order you to produce an accounting to be given to the beneficiaries. This is one of the most common orders made during estate litigation. The frequency of this type of order is not surprising, as too many executors persist in carrying on as if they do not have to report to anyone.

Usually a judge will allow 30 days for the executor to prepare the accounts and distribute copies to the beneficiaries who are entitled to receive them. On a similar note, a judge may order an executor to produce a better accounting than the one that has already been prepared, if he or she feels that efforts have been inadequate. See Chapter 12 for a detailed discussion of how to prepare an executor's accounting that will satisfy the beneficiaries, and if necessary, the court.

Producing an accounting does not have to be a burden if you keep proper records from the start. If you start properly at the beginning of the estate and maintain your records consistently, you will not be faced with a huge task when an accounting is required. Every executor knows — or should know — that sooner or later he or she will have to account to the beneficiaries and might even have to account to the court. Since you know that from the start, it only makes sense to set up the system that works the best and saves the most time for you.

It is a mistake to think that when it is time to prepare the accounting, you will be able to rely on your memory for details.

If you are required to produce an accounting and simply feel that the task is overwhelming, you are entitled to hire an accountant to help you with this and to charge the accountant's fees to the estate.

3. Requirement to Pass Accounts

A variation on the previous order may also be made. The judge may order that you bring your accounts to the courts for review rather than to the beneficiaries. This may be nerve-wracking for you, as you will have to present all paperwork to the judge and be prepared to answer any and all questions the court might have. Even with a lawyer present to represent you, the judge may direct questions your way.

The term "passing of accounts" refers to the process of the judge examining your executor's accounting and deciding whether it is acceptable. Passing the accounts is not automatic, as the judge will examine any individual entries about which the beneficiaries may have complained. Many an executor has been sent away with instructions to come back a week later to show the judge a significantly better set of paperwork. Most estates do not end up with a court passing of accounts unless there is a dispute over the accounting that simply cannot be resolved between the executor and beneficiaries.

If you and the beneficiaries are disagreeing about how much you may take as executor's compensation, you may well find yourself passing your accounts with the court to explain why you are entitled to that fee.

It is worthwhile to note that not every passing of accounts is initiated by the beneficiaries, as the courts are available to assist any party to an estate. Sometimes the executor's accounts are reviewed by the courts at the request of the executor. You might ask the court to review your accounts if the beneficiaries refuse to sign release documents that approve your accounts and executor's fee. Regardless of who initiates the court action, the court will decide whether the accounting is complete and whether your fee is appropriate.

4. Reduction of the Executor's Compensation

If there has been a financial loss to the estate, the judge may order that the fee you plan to take from the estate is to be reduced by the amount of the loss, or completely taken away from you. This is more likely to happen in the event you have been careless or negligent than if you are involved in intentional fraud or theft, which would likely result in more serious repercussions.

A general rule across Canada is that an executor may claim up to 5 per cent of the estate as a fee, and claim reimbursement of reasonable out-of-pocket expenses as well. See Chapter 12, sections **4.** and **5.** of this book for a detailed discussion on how to calculate your fee, and a discussion about claiming appropriate expenses.

If beneficiaries do not agree to the amount you wish to be paid, the matter may be decided by the courts, generally along with a passing of accounts. Then you will have to justify your claim to the judge. It is fair to say that if the judge believes that your actions or lack of action has caused a loss to the estate, he or she is not likely to allow you the full executor's fee.

Some examples of the kind of losses that would be set off against the fee you would otherwise expect to receive include:

- Capital gains tax that must be paid on the sale of the family residence because you held it in the name of the estate for too long.

- Loss of interest income on funds that you failed to invest.

- Excessive payments to helpers.

- The funds that were not received because you sold an estate asset too cheaply.

5. Removal of the Executor

A judge has the power to remove you from your executor's duties completely and to appoint someone else in your place. This is certainly a popular request by beneficiaries, as each of them may think (rightly or wrongly) that he or she could have done a better job of it than you have done. Removal of an executor is considered by the courts to be fairly drastic action, as they generally do not like to override wishes left by the deceased. The court will try not to interfere with the way the deceased has set up things, and the decisions made by the deceased, if at all possible.

However, if your behaviour is really egregious, or the losses are mounting up, or if there is so much bickering between you and the beneficiaries that nothing can be accomplished, you could be removed as executor. This is the action that most beneficiaries say they want from the courts, though it may not always work the way they want it to. Beneficiaries who petition for an executor to be removed are likely angry at the executor and want to punish him or her. They usually expect the judge to appoint them in place of the existing executor.

In reality, the judge is not interested in humiliating an executor or getting in the middle of sibling rivalries. The judge is interested in having the estate wound up as efficiently and effectively as possible. Therefore, if the judge feels that this can be accomplished by an existing executor by giving that executor some rules, limits, or assistance, this is what will happen.

The court may not wish to replace one feuding sibling executor with another, as that may not solve the underlying issue. The feud would probably continue. The court may order that the Public Trustee, or a trust company (depending on the value of the estate) be put in charge of the estate rather than the executor or any of the beneficiaries. This is standard procedure where the family members simply cannot get along, to the detriment of the estate.

6. Requirement to Repay the Estate Personally

If there has been a financial loss to the estate, the judge may order you to repay the loss using your personal funds. This might happen, for example, if you sell an asset for less than fair market value, or fail to invest estate monies, or give estate assets to someone who is not a beneficiary. Doing any of those things causes the amount of money in the estate to be less, which means that the beneficiaries will inherit less. It is not your money you are losing; it is theirs.

Some of the ways in which executors cause a loss are less obvious than others. For example, if you file estate tax returns after the deadline, there may well be interest or penalties payable to Canada Revenue Agency. If the delay was your fault, you may be required to repay the interest and penalties to the estate. By the way, not knowing about deadlines or other tax and legal rules is not considered an excuse for not taking care of the estate as if you did know of them.

6.1 Order of costs/legal fees

You may already be aware that when a lawsuit has been heard in court, the parties involved are entitled to ask the judge to make an order about who is to pay the cost of the lawyers. In most litigation, including lawsuits involving the executor of an estate, the loser of the lawsuit must pay some or all of the winner's costs.

As a general rule, an executor's legal fees are paid from the estate as long as the executor is acting reasonably and the issue being litigated is one that was caused by the estate itself and not by the executor's actions. However, if you are faced with an application to be removed, or with theft or fraud allegations, you cannot expect that your fees will necessarily be paid by the estate. This is up to the judge, who will decide each case on its own facts. The judge may require you to pay not only your own legal fees, but the legal fees for the beneficiaries as well.

7. Contempt of Court

If a court has made any of the above orders, and you refuse or fail to carry out those orders, the judge may decide that you are in contempt of court. This could result in a monetary fine or a jail term for you.

This is unlikely to happen to you if you are doing all that you can to carry out the judge's order but are prevented from doing so by factors outside of your control. However, an executor who simply does not bother to do what the judge has ordered can expect punitive consequences. If a judge has given you an order and you find that you cannot fulfill it for some reason (the bank lost the paperwork and had to order a replacement copy from head office, or the appraiser you hired did not show up because he was ill), you are better off going back to the judge yourself before the deadline is up, and explaining yourself. At least that way the judge knows that you are doing what you can and not simply ignoring the situation.

In 2009, the Ontario court dealt with the *Willis Estate*. In that case, a person acting under a Power of Attorney for property for his mother was ordered by the court to pass his accounts and to provide an inventory of his mother's assets. The individual did not follow the order, even though he had sufficient time to do so, and ended up back in court. The judge found him to be in contempt of court for failing to do as he had been ordered. The man was ordered to pay a fine of $7,000 for his contempt. The judge went on to say that failure to pay the fine would lead to seven days in jail.

The *Willis Estate* is a good example of how the court will deal with contempt of court, as eventually even the most patient judge will get tired of an uncooperative executor. This procedure is not unique to estate litigation.

8. Criminal Charges

This particular remedy is different from all of the others listed above because it will only occur if your actions are severe enough to be the cause of criminal charges. In the vast majority of cases, executors can be dealt with by the civil courts in the ways described above. However, if you have stolen or embezzled funds from an estate or from a trust that is part of an estate, you may be charged with theft or fraud, depending on the facts. This could result in a jail term for you.

This is certainly not common in estates, as most never make the leap from civil lawsuits to criminal law charges. However, over the last few years, courts have started to crack down severely on executors who help themselves to estate assets or trust funds. It has become obvious that some executors and administrators are more than willing to help themselves to estate or trust funds, and the courts are responding as can be expected.

Theft by an executor is not the same as theft by a stranger. It is considered worse, because not only does the executor steal the funds or property, but he or she also violates the position of trust given by the deceased. This means that the punishment for theft by an executor or administrator would be harsher than the punishment would be for theft of the same amount of money by a stranger.

15
Issues Specific to Estate Administrators

In many respects, a court-appointed administrator is the same as an executor. They have the same job to do, the same legal obligations to the estate, and are entitled to the same compensation. However, the big difference in terms of protection from liability is in the fact that an administrator is not appointed by the will, and therefore must wait until a court appoints him or her before getting started working on the estate.

An executor named in a will has the legal right to begin representing the estate as soon as the deceased has passed away. That authority arises from the will document itself and not from an order of probate. The administrator, on the other hand, has no such authority. He or she is not legally entitled to do anything for the estate or even call himself or herself the administrator until that court order has been issued.

This difference manifests itself in several situations. Whereas an executor can walk into the deceased's bank or investment broker with a copy of the will and give instructions about the account, the administrator must wait for the court process to authorize him or her to do that. This chapter takes a closer look at some of the situations in which an administrator is in a different position from an executor, and must behave differently to avoid legal complications.

1. Funeral, Burial, or Cremation Arrangements

An executor who is appointed by a will has the legal right to make all decisions with respect to the deceased's funeral, burial or cremation arrangements. It has long been entrenched in the law of estates that these decisions are up to the executor, even if the executor is not the next of kin, or even a family member of the deceased. The right to make these arrangements arises from the will.

When there is no will and the courts must appoint an administrator, the same right to make decisions arises, but in reality the deceased's remains have already been dealt with before the courts appoint an administrator. Unless there is an investigation into the death, a deceased person is usually buried or cremated within a few days of death. The legal system does not work that quickly.

If you plan to be the administrator, have sent in your paperwork to the court and are waiting for the application to be processed, you are still not yet appointed as administrator. Therefore you will have to accede to the next of kin and allow them to make decisions about burial or cremation for the deceased.

2. Preparing an Inventory

If you are an administrator of an estate, you will feel the effects of the inconvenience of working without a will in the preparation of the estate inventory. In order to get a court order appointing you as administrator, you must apply to the court with a package of documents that includes an inventory of the estate. However, you have no legal authority to approach a bank, broker, or realtor on behalf of the estate until you have the court order. You need information in order to apply to the court for the right to get that information. It can be pretty frustrating.

Because of privacy laws across Canada, the job of the administrator has become more difficult. If you cannot obtain current information from banks, land registries, and insurance companies, you will have to do the best you can using the information you find at the deceased's home and workplace.

The inventory that is prepared under these circumstances is much less likely to be complete and accurate than it would be had the same inventory been prepared by an appointed executor. However, the job is not impossible. If you find that current information about assets is simply not available, you should describe that asset in the inventory and estimate the value. Make sure you include the word "estimate" if it is an estimate, because you will be required to swear under oath that the values you have applied in the inventory are correct.

For example, let us assume that your mother passed away without a will. You and your siblings agree that you will apply to the court to be named as administrator, so you begin the process of preparing the application. You find statements in your mother's kitchen drawer for a bank account, but the most recent statement is six months old. You cannot find out from the bank whether the account still exists, or what the value might be on the date your mother passed away.

From reading the statements, you discover that this is the account that your mother used for paying her bills. Her Old Age Security and Canada Pension Plan benefits were being deposited into the account. You are able to estimate the amounts that (assuming the account is still active) would have been deposited and withdrawn in the last six months, and to arrive at an approximate total. You think there should be about $78,000 in the account.

When you prepare the inventory, you describe the bank account, include the estimated total of $78,000, and put in the word "estimate" to indicate that you cannot back up this information with paperwork at the present time.

Occasionally an estate administrator, instead of using the word "estimate," will indicate on the inventory that a value is "to be determined." If you use that phrase, you are indicating to the court that you intend to file a supplemental affidavit with an updated inventory later on to provide that value. The court may insist that you do as you promised, and file another inventory. If you want to avoid being in that position, do not describe values as "to be determined."

If you find, after being appointed as administrator and obtaining new information, that the actual values are substantially different from those you estimated, you may wish to file a new inventory anyway. For example, you might have estimated that the account held $78,000, only to discover that your mother had paid for renovations to her home using that account, and that it now holds only $22,000. If the beneficiaries are not going to accept your word for it that the account was only $22,000, you might consider filing an amended inventory showing the new amount.

3. Applying for the CPP Death Benefit

One of the actions undertaken by an executor fairly early on in an estate administration is applying to Canada Pension Plan (CPP) for a death benefit. The benefit, which currently gives a maximum benefit of $2,500, is available to most Canadians, as long as they have worked for pay during their lives.

The application form asks for the identity of the person making the application. It contains a place for the legal representative of the estate to identify himself or herself. If you are the executor of the estate, you can fill that space in even if you are not going to apply for probate of the will. As an administrator, however, you cannot fill in that space unless you have been appointed by the court as the administrator.

This leaves you and the deceased's family with a choice to make. You may wait until the order appointing you has been made, and then apply for the CPP benefit. This would mean, of course, that there would be a much longer wait than usual for the death benefit to arrive.

Your other choice is for someone else in the family to apply for the benefit. This would most likely be a surviving spouse. This might be the right choice to make if the estate is very small or insolvent, and the CPP funds are required to help pay for the funeral.

4. Advertising for Creditors

Administrators, like executors, may choose to protect themselves by advertising in a local newspaper to find creditors and claimants against the estate (see Chapter 17 for more on this topic). The difference, however, is that an administrator may not place the advertisement until he or she has received the grant of administration from the court. This is because until the court approves of an administrator acting on behalf of the estate, he or she has no legal right to let others think he or she is in charge of the estate.

5. Listing the House for Sale

Generally speaking, real estate (including houses, raw land, cabins, rental properties, and mines and minerals titles) owned by a deceased person cannot be sold or transferred to the beneficiaries without a grant of probate or administration. This is because we are not allowed to sell property we do not own, and the courts and the land titles registry want proof that you are the legal representative of the deceased before you are allowed to sell any property belonging to the deceased.

An executor is allowed to list a property for sale before the grant of probate has been granted. If you do this, you must be very clear with potential buyers that you cannot transfer the title until probate is granted. However, you may still legally put up the listing, arrange for cleaning or repairs, show the property to prospective buyers, and sign the purchase agreement. In other words, all but the final title transfer may be done while waiting for the probate document.

An administrator is in a completely different position. If you are an administrator, you must wait for your grant of administration from the court before you list the property or even speak to a realtor. You cannot do anything related to the property yet; you may not in any way hold yourself out as being a representative of the estate until you have that document. To do otherwise is fraudulent.

6. Intestacy

At the root of the difference between executors and administrators is the fact that a court-appointed administrator almost never has a will to follow. It is possible, but fairly rare, that a valid will exists without an executor, in which case an administrator may be appointed to carry out that will. However, in the vast majority of cases, the administrator must deal with provincial or territorial intestacy laws.

Do not ever assume that you know what the law says about intestacy based on what your friends have told you, or you have seen on television, or even have read on a law blog. Either hire a lawyer to advise you as to what the law says, or look it up yourself. You must have accurate information.

Intestacy laws vary between provinces and territories. In some cases the differences are surprisingly large. What they all have in common is that they leave some portion of the estate to the spouse of the deceased, and some portion to the children of the deceased. That seems simple enough, but that simplicity can be deceptive when you try to apply it to a real, living family.

An error that trips up some administrators (and sometimes, executors) is assuming that the beneficiaries of the estate are the deceased's current, immediate family. Sometimes administrators overlook the fact that on intestacy, all biological children of the deceased are included in the distribution to children. If the deceased had a child of a previous marriage, or had a child out of wedlock, that biological child is entitled to the same share as a child who was born in the deceased's current marriage. This is true even where the deceased had little or no contact or relationship with that child.

You must ensure that before you make any distribution, you make detailed enquiries about any and all biological children who might exist. If you miss someone and pay out the estate without paying that person, you may be required to pay that child's share out of your own funds.

Children who have been legally adopted by the deceased are considered to be the children of the deceased for all legal purposes, which of course includes inheritances. They are treated exactly the same as biological children of the deceased by the law.

The opposite side of the coin also applies. When the biological parent of a child dies, but the child had been legally adopted by someone else, that child is no longer entitled to a share of the biological parent's estate. He or she is considered in law as no longer being that biological parent's child. Unfortunately, many children who have been adopted and later find their biological parents and re-establish a relationship believe that they are entitled to share in that parent's estate. They are incorrect, and if you as the executor or administrator distribute a share to a child who was adopted by someone else, you will end up paying that share back to the estate using your own money.

Also be aware that any distribution under intestacy does not include stepchildren. In these days of blended families, many people make completely unsupported assumptions about protections and rights afforded to them by law. Inheritance law is complicated and making assumptions is dangerous. Stepchildren do not have the same right to inherit that biological and adopted children have.

Imagine having to advise a bereaved spouse about these laws. You may have to tell a spouse that children he or she has never met will inherit a significant portion of the estate, while stepchildren that had been raised by the deceased will get nothing. It will be an unpleasant conversation, so make sure you are absolutely sure about the legalities before you go ahead.

16
Co-executor Liability

Co-executors are, by definition, people who work together on an estate, sharing the duties and responsibilities. They are supposed to work together at all times and be of one mind on decisions. An exception for the need for all decisions to be unanimous exists where the will contains a clause that allows executors to act by way of a majority vote.

However, unanimity is frequently impossible for co-executors to achieve. This is only to be expected when two or three very different people, each with his or her own idea of how best to deal with estate issues and his or her own priorities, are forced to work together. Personalities may clash violently, particularly where grief and shock over the loss of a loved one are factored in. The result may be co-executors who stop speaking to each other and carry on at cross purposes as if each of them were acting alone.

You will have to tread carefully if you are working as a co-executor with another person.

If you are dealing with a homemade will, you may find that several executors have been named to work together. Unfortunately, many people who make their own wills think it is a good idea to name all of their children as executors because they think this is a way of being fair. The end result is almost the same as not naming an executor at all, because when everyone is in charge, it is the same as having nobody in charge.

Most jurisdictions place a limit on how many executors may be named in a will, though this is not something that the general public may know or think about when making a will. The limit is usually three. Check the will that names you to see whether there are more than three named. If so, you will likely have to work out among yourselves who is going to act as executor and who is not. Hopefully you will be able to agree on this issue without resorting to the courts.

If you and your co-executor(s) intend to hire a lawyer to assist with the estate, it is a good idea to hire someone on whom you can agree. If at all possible, make sure that all co-executors attend all meetings with the lawyer and accountant. If it is not possible to be in the same physical location each time, consider holding calls using Skype or Google+.

This chapter looks at the question of whether you can incur personal liability because of the actions of a co-executor with whom you are working.

1. Renunciation

If you are named as the executor in a will, you do not have to accept the role. Turning down the job even though you are the person named is called renouncing your right to act as executor. Each province and territory allows for a named executor to renounce by doing so in writing in the proper form.

One of the main reasons executors refuse to take on the role is that they can see it is going to be a difficult task for them to carry out the estate administration, particularly alongside someone with whom they are not compatible, and they simply do not want the headaches. They do not want to risk the liability that is quite likely to arise if disagreements between co-executors end up in court. Having read the earlier chapters of this book, you may feel more prepared to handle those risks. However, if you do not wish to take on the job of executor, you are entitled to renounce.

You are allowed to renounce for any reason; it does not have to be because you do not want to risk personal liability. You may renounce because you are ill, because you are required to travel a lot with your regular job, or simply because you cannot manage the time required by the estate between your regular obligations.

There are rules attached to renouncing, and they are strict. A rule that is carved into legal stone is that you can only renounce at the very beginning of the estate, before you do anything to act as executor, or to make people think you are acting as the executor. The law refers to taking steps as executor even though you plan to renounce as "intermeddling." If you decide to renounce, you will have to do so in writing using the proper document, and part of that document will be a sworn statement that you have not intermeddled in the estate.

If the courts believe that you have intermeddled, you may not be allowed to renounce as executor. Any liability attached to the administration, or lack of administration, of the estate would therefore still attach to you, even if you discontinue doing anything for the estate.

Canadian courts have looked at a number of cases to decide what is intermeddling and what is not. It is clear from those cases that if all you do is pay some of the deceased's bills, you will not necessarily be seen to be intermeddling. This is particularly true of paying for the funeral, as this is often done by family members. In other words, paying for the funeral will not automatically mean to the court that you intend to carry on as executor.

If, however, you go to the bank or the land registry or the lawyer's office and represent yourself as being the executor, you will be seen to be intermeddling. You may go to the lawyer's office to discuss what would be involved in carrying out the estate and still renounce, as long as you have not taken any steps on behalf of the estate.

Once you start the job of executor, you are not allowed to quit unless you apply to the court for permission to do so. If the court is considering granting your request, it will require you to pass your accounts first. Therefore, you should think carefully about the job ahead of you before you jump in and start working on the estate. The court may not allow you to back out.

If you are acting as an executor and later on you want to quit, you will have to give your explanation to the court, which may or may not agree to let you off the hook. If you are moving out of the country or are extremely ill, the court will probably allow your application once it hears your evidence. Any executor who voluntarily quits will be required by the court to pass his or her accounts first, so that the court can ensure that all is in order before someone else takes over as executor.

2. Legal Protection

Assuming that you decide that renunciation is not the appropriate step for you to take, you will likely wonder how the activities of co-executors on behalf of the estate will impact each other. After all, you cannot control everything that the other co-executor will do.

There is some protection afforded to you by the law. The general rule is that a co-executor can only be held liable for his or her own actions, for the assets he or she actually received, or for his or her own omissions or errors. This rule is intended to protect a co-executor who is not aware that his or her co-executor has embezzled funds, has speculated foolishly with estate investments, or has made careless errors. It would also protect you if your co-executor sold assets at an undervalued price without your consent.

The law protects an executor who in good faith places estate assets with a bank or broker, when that bank or broker makes mistakes that lead to a loss to the estate. This is good news for an executor who is doing his or her best but cannot control the actions of others.

However, there is a caveat attached to these general rules. That exception is the concept of wilful default. It means that the executor who expects to be protected cannot just stay out of things entirely, leave all the work to his or her co-executor, and turn a blind eye to errors or fraud being carried out by the co-executor. The law refers to the kind of executor who does nothing at all as a "passive executor." The law does not allow a passive executor to give the co-executor free rein, then claim that he or she knew nothing about what was going on.

As an executor, you are required to participate in the estate administration and not just leave it in the hands of your co-executor. If you accept the job of executor but simply wash your hands of the estate (without formally renouncing), the courts will not be enthusiastic about protecting you.

17
More Ways to Protect Yourself

In this chapter, you will find several suggestions that are not specifically tied to any particular step or asset of the estate. These are ideas for reducing your personal liability as you consider the estate as a whole. They will affect your overall approach to the estate administration.

Not all ideas will be suitable for all executors, but it would be beneficial to consider each of them to decide whether it would be to your advantage to pursue each idea.

1. Direct the Deceased's Mail to Your Address

A task that you should do as early as possible in the estate administration is to go to the post office and redirect the deceased's mail to your own address. This will help you to locate assets and debts because you will receive bank statements, investment portfolio statements, credit card statements, and loan balance statements. It is an excellent source of information and will help ensure that you do not miss any assets or liabilities with which you must deal.

It is also important to do this so that other people do not have access to the deceased's personal information. Identity theft is rampant, and it happens fairly frequently to the deceased. As an executor, you are responsible for protecting the deceased's privacy and identity to the extent that is possible, so you want to make sure that you have not allowed unclaimed mail to accumulate where others can see it and access it.

Should the deceased's identity be stolen and used to commit fraud, and it was found that you had allowed paperwork to sit unguarded in the deceased's mailbox for weeks or months, you could well be on the hook for damages.

2. Advertise for Creditors and Claimants

Executors are not required by law to advertise in the newspaper to see whether there are any creditors of the deceased out there who have not been paid. So why do any of them bother to go to the time and expense of placing this kind of advertisement in the paper?

As discussed earlier in this book, an executor is required to pay all bills and expenses of the deceased and of the estate before any beneficiaries are paid. Certainly this includes bank loans and credit cards, but not all debts are so easy to discover. There could be anything from an unpaid housekeeper to a past due bill from the dentist.

If the executor pays the estate out to the beneficiaries and later finds out there is an outstanding bill or debt, he or she will most likely have to pay that bill himself or herself out of personal funds.

If, however, the executor places the advertisement in the local newspaper in accordance with the provincial or territorial rules, the executor may avoid this liability. The advertisement places a deadline, usually 30 days from the date of the advertisement, for anyone who believes they are owed money by the deceased to come forward and make the claim to the executor. If the would-be creditor does not reply in time and makes his or her claim known only after the estate has been paid out, the executor will not have to pay him or her personally.

After advertising, the executor will honestly be able to say that he or she did everything required to find out about outstanding debts, and did not deliberately ignore the possibility that other debts existed.

Each executor must assess for himself or herself whether it is a good idea to place this type of advertisement, as it does cost money to put a notice in the newspaper. The executor must decide whether there is a reasonable risk of any unknown creditors existing.

In some cases, an executor may be pretty sure there are no such creditors. This would certainly be the case if the executor had also been acting as the deceased's power of attorney before the deceased passed away, and felt that he or she was very familiar with all of the deceased's affairs. On the other extreme, the deceased might have been a business owner who ran his or her business as a sole proprietorship. In that case, there could well be several suppliers or customers who were owed money, especially if the deceased happened to be a poor record-keeper.

Most estates will fall somewhere in the middle of those two examples. As executor, you must look at the situation and make a realistic assessment of whether there is a risk of a creditor out there.

If you decide to place an advertisement, make sure you are following the local rules. Each province and territory has its own rules about probate and estate-related matters. The rules will describe the content of the advertisement, as well as how often the advertisement must run, the time that must elapse between sequential advertisements, and how long a creditor has to respond.

In order to ensure that you limit your liability, make sure you ask the staff at the newspaper for an Affidavit of Publication. Many of the daily newspapers in larger cities are asked this so often that their staff automatically produces them and sends them to executors. With smaller newspapers that may be less familiar with the process, you will likely have to prepare the Affidavit yourself (or ask the estate lawyer to do it) and send it to the newspaper to have their staff sign it.

The Affidavit of Publication is simply a sworn statement by the clerks at the newspaper that attaches a copy of the advertisement as it appeared in the paper, and describing exactly when it was published. Because it is in the form of an affidavit, it may be filed at the probate court if you wish, or if the court asks for it. This is your evidence that you advertised for creditors in accordance with the rules. This simple affidavit could save you from having to pay a creditor or claimant out of your own pocket.

3. Executor's Insurance

Executor's insurance is a relatively new insurance product that most executors have never heard of. It has only been around for a few years, but is available across Canada. Many wills and estates lawyers do not suggest this type of insurance, simply because they have always worked with executors who have carried on without it. It can be a slow process to change the way lawyers have done things for years, even when the change is an improvement. However, executor's insurance is now firmly in the sights of all wills lawyers.

However, it is the executor who carries the legal liability for the estate, so it is up to each executor to decide whether or not he or she wants to look into executor's insurance. This section of the book should give you at least enough information to decide whether you want to contact an insurance provider to find out more about it.

This type of policy is intended to protect an executor when a beneficiary starts a claim or lawsuit for which the executor might have to pay out of his or her own money. It covers that loss, as well as the cost of hiring a lawyer to defend you. The policy is purchased early on in the estate, before anything disruptive happens.

Buying this kind of insurance does not mean that you are planning to do a superficial job and you expect there might be trouble. In fact, if you do a sloppy job without even trying to get it right, even insurance will not help you. The policy is often attractive to executors who intend to do the best job they possibly can but can see that the estate might have issues. As you have seen by reading this book, it is difficult, if not impossible, to please all of the beneficiaries all of the time, and there is always a risk attached to acting as an executor.

Executor's insurance seems like a reasonable expense when an executor is hearing disputes and grumbles before he or she has even begun to get to work. Families fight during estates; that is simply a fact, and few families are immune. However, in some families the bickering is worse than in others, and a realistic executor has to wonder how much of that anger and dissatisfaction is going to be aimed his or her way.

Usually, an executor's insurance policy is paid for by the estate. So far, there have been no cases decided in the courts that rule on the issue of whether executor's insurance is properly paid for by the estate. However, the general rule for executors is that his or her costs are covered by the estate as long as those costs are of benefit to the estate.

The executor's point of view is that the policy does not just protect the executor. Without an insurance policy, it is possible that the cost of the executor's defence against the claim may be paid from the estate (depending on the outcome of the lawsuit). If that is the case, estate assets are used to pay those costs and the beneficiaries would inherit less. In this way, the policy benefits the beneficiaries of the estate as well, as the cost of the policy is certainly cheaper than the cost of a lawyer to defend the executor.

Beneficiaries may not realize that there is an executor's insurance policy in effect until they see the cost of the premiums on the executor's accounting. If they object to the premiums for the policy being paid from the estate, they will have the chance to say so when they are asked to sign the release.

The cost of buying this type of policy is not the same for every estate. The value of the estate is factored in. The amount of coverage requested is also factored in. The complexity of the case is also a factor, as it takes longer to wind up an estate that has complications such as unclear wording in the will, foreign assets to sell, or tax problems. However, providers of executor's insurance state that a three-year policy to cover an estate of $1,000,000 will cost about $2,000.

There is a tool called an Estate Risk Profile, used by ERAssure, a Canadian supplier of executor's insurance to let executors decide whether they want to look into buying this type of insurance. Considering the points on the profile will only take a few minutes, but it might get you thinking about risks on the estate you are administering and whether insurance would be worth it for you. See www.erassure. com/images/img/estate_risk_profile_m-100912-2013.pdf (accessed March 30, 2014).

4. Hire a Trust Company As Agent

Trust companies are the best-kept secrets in the wills and estates industry. Some people know that at the time you make your will, you can choose to name a trust company as an executor. What people do not generally know is that an executor who is looking after the estate of a deceased person can hire a trust company to do the work for him or her.

When an executor hires a trust company for help, the executor remains the executor; he or she does not abdicate that legal authority. While the executor remains the person who ultimately calls the shots, he or she does not have to personally perform tasks such as getting appraisals on property, cleaning out the deceased's home, filing tax returns, collecting in bank accounts and investments, writing to beneficiaries, or paying bills. In fact, a trust company will do as much or as little of the estate as the executor wants it to do.

The most common reason that executors seek this help from a trust company is that there are contentious family dynamics. Sometimes it is a blended family that cannot accommodate the other "half" of the family. At other times the problem is simply a group of beneficiaries that are quarrelling and perhaps threatening to sue the executor if things are not done their way. In other words, the executor can see what a huge headache the estate is going to be, and wants to remove himself or herself from the frontlines.

In other cases, the executor finds the estate too challenging, perhaps because the executor lives at a distance from where the deceased lived, or because the executor is already so busy with his or her own life. It can be really difficult to find the time to work on an estate when you work full time and care for a family.

When an executor hires a trust company as his or her agent to work on an estate, the fee for the trust company is taken out of the estate. The executor does not have to pay a fee up-front or provide a retainer. However, the executor should expect to reduce his or her executor's fee to reflect the fact that some of the work was delegated to someone else. This generally does not mean that the executor gets no fee at all, as the executor still carries the responsibility to see that the estate is finalized.

Executors and beneficiaries alike assume that trust companies are too expensive for ordinary people to hire. The fees vary from trust company to trust company, but they are much lower than most people believe. Contrary to popular belief, trust companies are not just for the wealthy. Policies regarding acceptable business will of course vary from one trust company to another, but estates as small as $250,000 may be administered.

Using a trust company can reduce the risk for an executor because the staff are trained and experienced with estates, and know which steps to take. The risk of a will being wrongly interpreted or an asset being improperly sold are minimal. Trust companies are highly regulated by the banking industry and have tools, personnel, and systems in place to properly safeguard an estate.

5. Get a Tax Clearance Certificate

A Tax Clearance Certificate is a document that is issued by Canada Revenue Agency to certify that an estate has paid all taxes and the residue can now be distributed to the beneficiaries. It will not be issued automatically; the executor must apply for it. If you are using an accountant to prepare tax returns for the estate, you may ask the accountant to request the certificate. Again, the accountant will not apply for the certificate without your knowledge or approval; it is up to you to request this.

You may apply for the certificate after the estate has been wound up. This means that you cannot apply for the certificate until all assets have been collected and all debts have been paid. Before applying, you must have completed all required tax returns, have received the Notice of Assessment from CRA for the returns, and paid the tax indicated on the Notice of Assessment. In larger or more complicated estates, an executor may request interim clearance certificates to cover certain periods of time, but in most estates there is only one certificate issued.

It is not required by law that you request the Tax Clearance Certificate. Most executors apply for it because it is the confirmation they need that no further taxes are owing, before they pay the beneficiaries. As has been mentioned many times in this book, it is a good idea to have back-up for the actions that you take as executor in order to reduce your personal liability, and a Tax Clearance Certificate is your back-up in terms of taxes.

It takes many months after applying for a Tax Clearance Certificate for it to arrive. Often, it takes a full year. Because of this, beneficiaries become impatient and suspicious, as they find it hard to believe that it really takes that long. Be prepared for this issue. Make sure you tell the beneficiaries during one of your regular reports that you have applied for the certificate. Manage their expectations by advising them that you expect it to take a minimum of six months for the certificate to arrive.

To obtain a Tax Clearance Certificate, you must file a Form TX19 (see Sample 7). The Canada Revenue Agency webpage has a fillable PDF form that you may find convenient.

Sample 7
Asking for a Tax Clearance Certificate (Forms TX19)

Canada Revenue Agency   **Agence du revenu du Canada**

ASKING FOR A CLEARANCE CERTIFICATE

Protected B
when completed

Use this form if you are the legal representative for an estate, business, or property and you are asking for a clearance certificate before distributing the assets of the estate, business, or trust. A legal representative includes an executor, administrator, liquidator, trustee, or like person other than a trustee in bankruptcy.

Send this form to the Assistant Director, Audit, at your tax services office. Do **not** attach this form to the tax return. You can find the address of your tax services office by going to **www.cra.gc.ca/contact**.

Do **not** send us this form until:

- you have filed all the required tax returns and have received the related notices of assessment; and
- we have received payment of (or have accepted security for) all income taxes (including the provincial or territorial taxes we administer), Canada Pension Plan contributions, employment insurance premiums, and any related interest and penalties.

Attach to this form the documents listed below to help us issue the certificate without delay:

- a copy of the will, including any codicils, renunciations, disclaimers, and all probate documents. If the taxpayer died intestate, also attach a copy of the document appointing an administrator (for example, the Letters of Administration or Letters of Verification issued by a probate court);
- a copy of the trust document for inter vivos trusts;
- a statement showing the list of assets and distribution plan, including a description of each asset, adjusted cost base, and the fair market value at the date of death and at the date of distribution, if not at the same time. Also include the names, addresses, and social insurance numbers or account numbers of the recipients as well as each one's relationship to the deceased. If a statement of properties has been prepared for a probate court, we will usually accept a copy, and a list of any properties that the deceased owned before death and that passed directly to beneficiaries;
- any other documents that are necessary to prove that you are the legal representative; and
- a letter of authorization that you have signed or a completed Form T1013, *Authorizing or Cancelling a Representative*, if you want us to communicate with any other person or firm, or you want the clearance certificate sent to any address other than your own.

For more information, refer to Information Circular IC82-6, *Clearance Certificate*, or call **1-800-959-8281**.

DO NOT USE THIS AREA

Identification area

Name of deceased, corporation, or trust, whichever applies

Address

Social insurance number, business number, or trust number, whichever applies	Date of death **or** date of wind-up, whichever applies

Legal representative's name (if there is more than one, please provide the details on a separate sheet)

Legal representative's address (we will send the clearance certificate to this address)

Legal representative's capacity (for example, executor, administrator, liquidator, or trustee)	Telephone number

---

Period covered

I am asking for a clearance certificate for the period ending _____

Tax returns filed

Have you filed any tax returns for the year of death?   ☐ Yes   ☐ No

If *yes*, indicate what type of tax return(s) you filed. For more information, get guides T4011, *Preparing Returns for Deceased Persons*, T4012, *T2 Corporation – Income Tax Guide*, and/or T4013, *T3 Trust Guide*.

☐ T1 final return   ☐ T1 return for rights or things   ☐ T2 Corporation Income Tax Return

☐ T1 return for income from a testamentary trust   ☐ T1 return for partner or proprietor   ☐ T3 Trust Income Tax and Information Return

---

Certification and undertaking

I am asking for a clearance certificate from the Minister of National Revenue. The certificate will certify that all taxes (including provincial or territorial taxes administered by the Canada Revenue Agency), Canada Pension Plan contributions, employment insurance premiums, and any related interest and penalties for which the deceased, corporation, or trust named above is liable (or can reasonably be expected to become liable) have been paid or that the Minister has accepted security for the amounts. The certificate will apply to the tax year in which the distribution is made and any previous year for which I am liable (or can reasonably be expected to become liable) as the legal representative of the deceased, corporation, or trust identified. I will complete the distribution of all of the property as soon as possible after I receive the clearance certificate.

Date	Capacity (for example, executor, administrator, liquidator, or trustee)	Signature
Date	Capacity (for example, executor, administrator, liquidator, or trustee)	Signature

Privacy Act, personal information bank number CRA PPU 015

TX19 (13)

Canadá

The Download Kit

Please enter the link information you see in the box below into your computer web browser to access and download the kit.

www.self-counsel.com/updates/avoid/kit14.htm

The download kit includes:

- Executor's Ledger

- Checklist of Executor's Duties

- Statement of Reccipts and Disbursements

- Statement of Proposed Disbursements

- Statement of Proposed Executor's Compensation

- Provincial Probate Registries

- Estate-Related Statutes by Province and Territories, with the Exception of Québec